Marine Tourism, Climate Change, and Resilience in the Caribbean, Volume I

Marine Tourism, Climate Change, and Resilience in the Caribbean, Volume I

Ocean Health, Fisheries, and Marine Protected Areas

Edited by
Kreg Ettenger, PhD
With Samantha Hogenson
Center for Responsible Travel (CREST)

BEP BUSINESS EXPERT PRESS

CREST
Center for Responsible Travel

Marine Tourism, Climate Change, and Resilience in the Caribbean,
Volume I: Ocean Health, Fisheries, and Marine Protected Areas
Copyright © Business Expert Press, LLC, 2017.
Center for Responsible Travel (CREST), 2017.

First published in 2017 by
Business Expert Press, LLC
222 East 46th Street, New York, NY 10017
www.businessexpertpress.com

Center for Responsible Travel (CREST)
1225 Eye Street, NW, Suite 600
Washington, DC 20005

ISBN-13: 978-1-63157-751-2 (paperback)
ISBN-13: 978-1-63157-752-9 (e-book)

Business Expert Press Tourism and Hospitality Management Collection

Collection ISSN: 2375-9623 (print)
Collection ISSN: 2375-9631 (electronic)

Cover and interior design by S4Carlisle Publishing Services
Private Ltd., Chennai, India

First edition: 2017

10 9 8 7 6 5 4 3 2 1

Printed in the United States of America.

Dedication

For the innovative leaders in sustainable tourism who have seen the realities of climate change and are proactively working to find solutions.

Abstract

As the island and coastal nations of the Caribbean respond to and prepare for the effects of climate change, tourism has the potential to both exacerbate and mitigate these effects. In the four volumes of this collection, we look at the role of coastal and marine tourism in the Caribbean and several similar regions, considering the impacts of the tourism sector on marine and coastal environments and on the biological and human communities that depend on them. We also explore the way the tourism industry is responding to climate change, and how various sectors are adapting and preparing for the changes yet to come. Through essays and case studies by scientists, entrepreneurs, NGO leaders, and resource managers, we show that marine and coastal tourism have the ability to lead the way when it comes to reducing human-induced climate impacts, protecting and restoring crucial ecosystems and habitats, and building sustainable futures for the people of the Caribbean and beyond.

In this book, the third of four volumes, we look specifically at marine tourism and its connections with ocean health, fisheries, and critical ecosystems including coral reefs. We also consider the important role that marine protected areas can play in preserving coral reefs and other ecosystems, leading to greater resilience in the face of the environmental and economic impacts of climate change. Finally, we look at some examples of how the tourism industry is responding to climate change, using its economic and social capital to foster positive change in the Caribbean and other parts of the world.

Keywords

Caribbean, climate change, marine tourism, responsible tourism, sustainable tourism, ocean health, fisheries, marine protected areas, sustainable development, adaptation, resilience, mitigation

Contents

Foreword and Acknowledgments

The idea for this volume on marine tourism, and its three companion volumes, grew out of the 2015 "Innovators Think Tank: Climate Change and Coastal & Marine Tourism," held in Punta Cana, Dominican Republic, July 22–24, 2015. Organized and hosted by the Center for Responsible Travel (CREST) and the Grupo Puntacana Foundation, the Think Tank brought together some 35 sustainable tourism practitioners and climate change experts to take stock of how coastal and marine tourism in the Caribbean are dealing with climate change and its impacts, and to identify priorities that need to be addressed. Our discussions, ably facilitated by Roger-Mark De Souza of the Woodrow Wilson Center, were organized around a single critical theme: *How coastal and marine tourism must be planned, built, and operated in this era of climate change.*

One outcome of the Think Tank was the unanimous decision to put together a publication on the same theme as a tool for public education. We are grateful that many of the Think Tank participants agreed to contribute essays and case studies for these four volumes. Additional authors were identified during the year that we have worked on the books. All generously contributed their expertise to this common project.

Early in the process, Kreg Ettenger, associate professor in the Department of Anthropology at the University of Maine, agreed to come on board as editor of the marine tourism volumes. His contributions have been enormous and have added greatly to the quality of the books. Indispensable as well to this project has been Samantha Hogenson, CREST's managing director, who not only contributed to the concept and content, but also, with her usual efficiency, oversaw the final copy editing and assembling of the manuscript.

She also oversaw the CREST researchers who have worked diligently on numerous essential but often tedious details. Patricia Nuñez Garcia, who was part of the CREST team at the Think Tank, transcribed a number of presentations that have been reshaped into contributions for the manuscript. Ashley Newson and Helena Servé organized all the photos and graphics, including successfully securing permissions for each of them. Helena also stepped in to assist with numerous research tasks as well as some of the copyediting. Finally, four other CREST researchers, Gabriela Aguerrevere Yanez, Angela Borrero, Emily Simmons, and Noora Laukkanen, contributed to tracking down information, researching topics, and identifying potential authors. We are grateful to this entire team!

We would like to thank Scott Isenberg and Business Expert Press for taking an early interest in our proposal and agreeing to publish these volumes. We were fortunate to make contact just as BEP was launching its Tourism and Hospitality Management Collection, and to find that, like CREST, BEP focuses on reaching academic and business audiences. We are also grateful to the collection editor, Dr. Betsy Stringam of New Mexico State University, for her helpful comments and enthusiastic reception of our manuscripts.

We thank these contributors and collaborators one and all, and hope that they will be as pleased with the final product as we are at CREST.

—Martha Honey
CREST Executive Director

Key Definitions

Adaptation: The adjustment in natural or human systems in response to actual or expected climatic stimuli or their effects, which moderates harm or exploits beneficial opportunities.[1]

Caribbean: According to the United Nations, the Caribbean region consists of: Anguilla, Antigua and Barbuda, Aruba, The Bahamas, Barbados, Bonaire, Saint Eustatius and Saba, British Virgin Islands, Cayman Islands, Cuba, Curaçao, Dominica, Dominican Republic, Grenada, Guadeloupe, Haiti, Jamaica, Martinique, Montserrat, Puerto Rico, Saint-Barthélemy, Saint Kitts and Nevis, Saint Lucia, Saint Vincent and the Grenadines, Saint-Martin (French) and Sint Maarten (Dutch), Trinidad and Tobago, Turks and Caicos Islands, and United States Virgin Islands.[2]

Marine Protected Area: The International Union for the Conservation of Nature and Natural Resources (IUCN) defines a protected area as "A clearly defined geographical space, recognised, dedicated and managed, through legal or other effective means, to achieve the long-term conservation of nature with associated ecosystem services and cultural values." Marine protected areas come under a variety of names and with a wide range of purposes and levels of protection, as described in the IUCN's 2012 guidelines on the subject.[3] The Convention on Biological Diversity, in its COP 7 Decisions in 2004, expanded the term to "Marine and Coastal Protected Areas" (MCPAs) to include adjacent coastal areas, which are often important components of critical marine ecosystems.[4]

Marine Tourism: Those recreational activities that involve travel away from one's place of residence and which have as their host or focus the marine environment.[5]

Mitigation: The lessening or limitation of the adverse impacts of hazards and related disasters.[6]

Resilience: The ability to prepare and plan for, absorb, recover from, and more successfully adapt to adverse events.[7]

Responsible Tourism: Tourism that maximizes the benefits to local communities, minimizes negative social or environmental impacts, and helps local people conserve fragile cultures and habitats or species.[8]

Sustainable Development: Development that meets the needs of the present without compromising the ability of future generations to meet their own needs.[9]

Sustainable Tourism: Tourism that leads to the management of all resources in such a way that economic, social, and aesthetic needs can be fulfilled while maintaining cultural integrity, essential ecological processes, biological diversity, and life support systems.[10]

Notes

1. The United Nations Office for Disaster Risk Reduction. (2009). *Terminology.* Available at: https://www.unisdr.org/we/inform/terminology.

2. United Nations Department of Economic and Social Affairs. (2016). *Composition of macro geographical (continental) regions, geographical sub-regions, and selected economic and other groupings.* UN Statistics Division. Available at: http://unstats.un.org/unsd/methods/m49/m49regin.htm.

3. Jon Day, et al. (2012). *Guidelines for Applying the IUCN Protected Area Management Categories to Marine Protected Areas.* Gland, Switzerland: IUCN, 36 pp. Available at: https://portals.iucn.org/library/node/10201, (accessed September 30, 2016).

4. Convention on Biological Diversity. (2004). *Seventh Ordinary Meeting of the Conference of the Parties to the Convention on Biological Diversity, February 9-20, 2004, Kuala Lumpur, Malaysia.* Available at: https://www.cbd.int/decisions/cop/?m=cop-07.

5. Mark Orams. (1999). *Marine Tourism: Development, Impacts and Management.* London: Routledge, 132 pp.

6. United Nations Office for Disaster Risk Reduction. (2009). Op cit.

7. Urban Land Institute Center for Sustainability. (2015). *Returns on Resilience: The Business Case.* Washington, D.C.: The Urban Land Institute. Available at: http://uli.org/wp-content/uploads/ULI-Documents/Returns-on-Resilience-The-Business-Case.pdf, (accessed September 16, 2016).

8. City of Cape Town. (August 2002). *Cape Town Declaration.* Cape Town Conference on Responsible Tourism in Destinations. Available at: https://www.capetown.gov.za/en/tourism/Documents/Responsible%20Tourism/Toruism_RT_2002_Cape_Town_Declaration.pdf, (accessed September 20, 2016).

9. World Commission on Environment and Development. (1987). *Our Common Future.* Oxford: Oxford University Press. Available at: http://www.un-documents.net/our-common-future.pdf

10. United Nations Sustainable Development Knowledge Platform. (2016). *Sustainable Tourism.* Available at: https://sustainabledevelopment.un.org/topics/sustainabletourism

List of Acronyms

CHTA—Caribbean Hotel & Tourism Association

CAST—Caribbean Alliance for Sustainable Tourism

CaMPAM—Caribbean Marine Protected Areas Managers

CICESE—Center for Scientific Research and Higher Education at Ensenada

CPI—Counterpart International

CPNP—Cabo Pulmo National Park

CSFs—Community Supported Fisheries

DHWs—Degree Heating Weeks

EAF—Ecosystem Approach to Fisheries

FAO—United Nations Food and Agriculture Organization

FIPs—Fishery Improvement Projects

FTAP—Fisheries Technical Assistance Program

GEARNET—Gear Conservation Engineering and Demonstration Network

GIZ—Deutsche Gesellschaft für Internationale Zusammenarbeit

GLA—Global Leadership Adventures

GMRI—Gulf of Maine Research Institute (Portland, Maine)

GPCF—Grupo Puntacana Foundation

GPS—Global Positioning System

ICCAS—Integrated Climate Change Adaptation Strategies

IUCN—International Union for the Conservation of Nature and Natural Resources

MDPI—Masyarakat dan Perikanen Indonesia (Communities and Fisheries of Indonesia)

MPAs—Marine Protected Areas

MREP—Marine Resource Education Program

NOAA—U.S. National Oceanic and Atmospheric Administration

NTMMB—Northern Telescope Mangrove Management Board (Grenada)

PADI—Professional Association of Diving Instructors

PESCA—Partnership for Ecologically Sustainable Coastal Areas

PCRC—Puntacana Resort and Club

SIDS—Small Island Developing States

SPAs—Sanctuary Preservation Areas

TAMR—Turneffe Atoll Marine Reserve

TASA—Turneffe Atoll Sustainability Association

UNESCO—United Nations Educational, Scientific, and Cultural
    Organization

ZOFEMAT—La Zona Federal Marítima Terrestre (Federal Maritime
    Land Zone, Mexico)

Map of the Caribbean

Map of the Caribbean Sea and its islands.

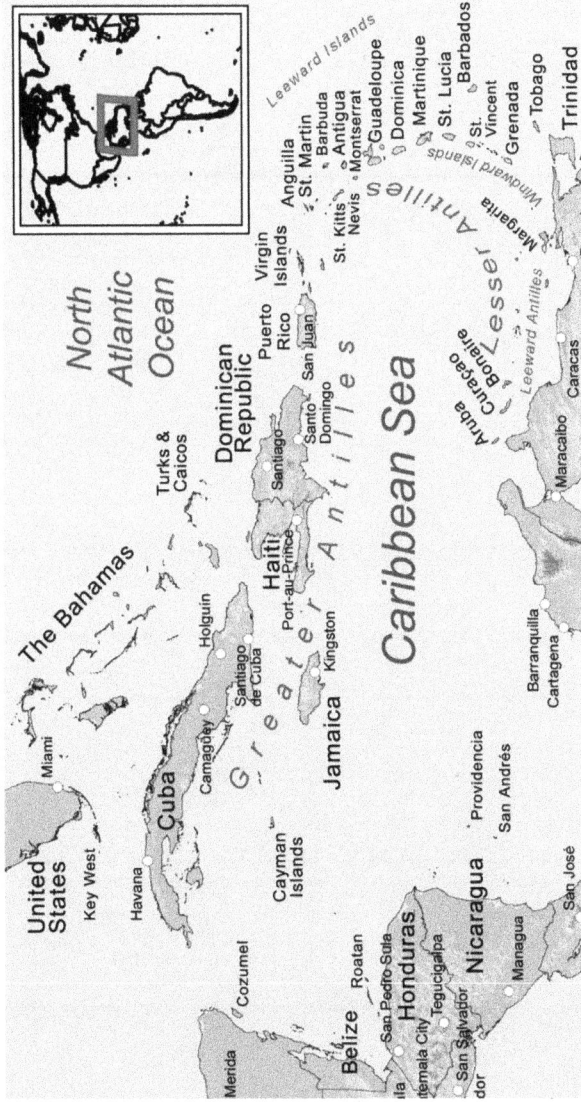

Source: Karl Musser, Creative Commons

CHAPTER 1

Introduction

Kreg Ettenger

This book looks at the complex relationship between climate change, tourism, oceans, and coastal communities, with a focus on the small island states of the Caribbean. Together with the three other volumes in this collection, it provides a current picture of the state of coastlines and waters in the Caribbean region, including how they support local communities through marine resources and tourism, the impacts of climate change on tourism as well as on ecosystems and coastal communities, and how tourism both contributes to and can potentially help mitigate climate impacts. For comparison, we also draw upon examples from other regions that share similarities with the Caribbean, including a reliance on marine resources and tourism.

The central theme of all four volumes is how coastal and marine tourism can and must be sustainably planned, built, and operated in this era of climate change. The authors, many of whom attended the Center for Responsible Travel's "Innovators Think Tank on Climate Change and Coastal & Marine Tourism" in July 2015, include tourism business owners, academics, scientists, community and nonprofit leaders, and government managers and employees. The key questions these authors explore include:

- How do various sectors of marine and coastal tourism contribute to climate change?
- How are these sectors experiencing the impacts of climate change?

- What measures have tourism businesses, governments, and other stakeholders taken already to address climate change and its impacts?
- Given the predicted future impacts of climate change, what are the main gaps between current and best practices by tourism businesses in addressing climate change?

In all four books, we take a practical and applied approach to these issues, focusing on solutions and best practices rather than simply identifying problems or accusing likely culprits. While we certainly acknowledge the seriousness of the issues at hand and the role that some industries, including tourism, have played in contributing to these problems, we believe the only way to move forward is to find solutions that work for multiple stakeholders and can achieve broad and strong support.

The first two books in this series, *Coastal Tourism, Sustainability, and Climate Change in the Caribbean: Volumes 1 and 2*, explore issues most relevant to coastal tourism destinations and activities, including beach and shoreline protection; tourism facility siting and development; sustainable hospitality operations; golf course design and management; airports and ground transportation; and agriculture and land-based food systems. In this book, we explore the health of ocean ecosystems, especially coral reefs, in the face of climate change; the state of ocean fisheries; and the importance of marine protected areas and their relation to tourism. In the fourth volume, we look at the marine recreation sector, including surfing, sport fishing, and diving; the cruise industry, including port destinations; and the yachting and marina sector.

Each chapter in this volume contains an overview essay that provides context for a particular issue. Following these are case studies describing particular settings, activities, or businesses. Many include information on what has worked to provide an additional measure of resilience in the face of current and projected impacts of climate change in this region. Given the wide range of examples available to us, we have selected only a few for each issue, but we hope these serve to illustrate some of the innovative ways in which communities, businesses, NGOs, government agencies, and others are responding to climate change. The following is an overview of each chapter to help guide the reader to the issues that interest them most.

Chapter 2: Coral Reefs and Marine Ecosystems in the Face of Climate Change

To begin, we look at ocean health and marine resources as the basis for a vital tourism economy—not to mention a requirement of viable coastal and island communities. Climate change is having marked impacts on many parts of the ocean ecosystem, from the quality of water itself (including temperature, acidity, and oxygen levels) to specific habitats like coral reefs and seagrass beds, to individual species from seaweed to zooplankton to game fish. This chapter describes the kinds of changes now taking place, focusing on two critical biomes, coral reefs and mangroves, both of which are being severely impacted by climate change and other factors. The chapter concludes with a discussion of a new problem that may also be climate-related: masses of sargassum seaweed washing up on beaches and choking bays in recent years.

The chapter begins with an overview essay on the current state of coral reefs in the Caribbean, which are under enormous threat from a number of stressors, including climate change. The essay is excerpted from an IUCN report that involved the most comprehensive study to date of the various factors affecting coral reefs across the Caribbean. The authors, Rubén Torres and Jeremy Jackson, explain that most of the factors leading to recent dramatic declines in coral reef health are human-induced, including overfishing, population growth, rapid development of coastal areas, and invasive species. Warming ocean temperatures add to these stresses and make it more difficult for reefs to survive and recover when they are damaged by storms, disease, and other threats. As a result, coral reefs in the Caribbean, as in many places around the world, are facing an uncertain future, as are those who depend on them for food, storm protection, and tourism activities.

Turning toward more positive ideas, a case study by Victor Galvan and Jake Kheel looks at a successful coral reef restoration project that has incorporated local fishers and recreational divers as participants in coral gardening and replanting efforts. The project is a collaboration between several partners including the Grupo Puntacana Foundation, an offshoot of the Puntacana Resort and Club. A second case study, by Dieter Rothenberger and Aria St Louis, looks at restoration of mangroves, another vital ecosystem under threat from climate change and other factors. Their project in Telescope, Grenada, involves local community members and has resulted in the planting of over one thousand mangrove seedlings in just the first year.

The final case study in this chapter looks at a new and emerging threat in the Caribbean: the increasing waves of sargassum seaweed that have arrived on area beaches. This relatively new phenomenon, as described by Jake Kheel and Kreg Ettenger, may be related to climate change and specifically to warmer waters and shifting ocean currents that are bringing dense wracks of seaweed onto Caribbean beaches, affecting wildlife and tourists alike. This is just one example of how climate change may already be affecting the Caribbean, disrupting ecosystems and putting local economies at risk.

Chapter 3: Fisheries, Tourism, and Climate Change

Marine fisheries and tourism are connected in multiple ways, although those connections might not always be obvious. At the most immediate level, tourists have to eat, and many island and coastal visitors prefer to eat locally sourced seafood as part of their travel experience. A lack of ample fish and other marine-based foods in tourism destinations, the perception of diminished quality or selection, or the knowledge that such foods are imported from other areas can all detract from the visitor experience. In addition, local resorts and restaurants may find it more difficult and expensive to provide preferred seafood to customers, impacting their bottom line.

Sport fishing, spear fishing, snorkeling, scuba diving, and other marine recreation activities also rely on healthy and diverse fish populations, including game fish for anglers. Just as importantly, if not more so, the communities that support the tourism industry throughout the Caribbean and other island and coastal regions often depend heavily on locally harvested fish and other seafood for subsistence. In short, healthy fish populations in both nearshore and offshore areas are critical to a viable marine tourism industry, as well as to local communities. The authors in this chapter explore this issue and consider how climate change and other human factors are affecting world fisheries, and what impacts this could have on communities and the tourism industry.

The chapter begins with an overview by Dawn Martin of Ceres and Marida Hines of The Ocean Foundation. Their essay describes the current state of the world's fisheries, how climate change is compounding other problems such as overfishing and pollution, and the role that tourism can play in raising awareness about these issues. As the authors point out, global per capita fish consumption is rising along with total population, placing increasing pressure on the world's already dwindling fish stocks. In addition, climate change appears to be affecting the world's fisheries in many ways, from damaging coral reefs and other important fish nurseries and habitats to changing where various species can live and how well they can reproduce.

Not all of the news is bad, however. The authors point out that the commercial fishing industry, as well as governments and NGOs, are taking steps to protect the future of fishing and fish stocks. The tourism industry is also beginning to take steps toward more sustainable fisheries, with some independent resorts and restaurants, as well as large corporations like Marriott, now offering sustainable seafood options on their menus. The authors conclude by arguing that tourism itself, by placing people in direct contact with marine and coastal areas and introducing them to critical habitats and species, can foster attitudes and behaviors that might help ensure the future viability of fisheries for both food and recreational uses.

The two case studies in this chapter are not from the Caribbean, but do show how local communities, NGOs, and industry partners can work together to help create more resilient fisheries that might better withstand current and projected threats. The first case study describes a nongovernmental organization called Masyarakat dan Perikanen Indonesia (Communities and Fisheries of Indonesia) Foundation, or MDPI. The foundation has created partnerships with local fishing communities, as well as with global and regional partners like Anova Foods and the Balinese restaurant industry, to create and develop markets for sustainable seafood. The second case study talks about the Gulf of Maine Research Institute (GMRI) in Portland, Maine, USA. GMRI, a research and education organization, is working with commercial fishers, seafood buyers like grocery store chains, and the tourism industry to create a number of programs that help build more sustainable fisheries. MDPI and GMRI are on opposite sides of the globe but share many of the same goals, including creating demand for sustainably caught and processed seafood while supporting local fishing communities. They also employ similar strategies, especially forming partnerships between local fishing communities and the seafood and tourism industries.

Chapter 4: Marine Protected Areas as Climate Change Buffers and Tourism Magnets

The authors in Chapter 4 discuss the value of marine protected areas (MPAs) for preserving and restoring marine ecosystems, as well as their role in marine tourism. Chiara Zuccarino-Crowe of the U.S. National Oceanic and Atmospheric Administration (NOAA) first provides an overview of the role that MPAs can play in protecting critical ecosystems like coral reefs, and their potential for helping to ameliorate the regional and local impacts of climate change. As she points out, there are already some 500 MPAs across 38 countries in the wider Caribbean region, protecting an estimated total of 115,000 km^2, or 4 percent of the region's marine environments. Despite the relatively small proportion these protected areas represent geographically, they contribute significantly to the region's marine tourism economy, since a great deal of Caribbean diving activity is now focused on reefs found in MPAs.

One highly popular diving area is Turneffe Atoll, located some 30 miles east of Belize City and part of the Mesoamerican Reef System. Authors Craig Hayes and Kristin Kovalik, both with the Turneffe Atoll Trust, describe the process of creating the Turneffe Atoll Marine Reserve, which at 325,412 acres (131,690 ha) is Belize's largest marine reserve. Consultations about the reserve involved over 10,000 person-hours of meetings with local fishers and other stakeholders, many of whom were initially opposed to the reserve. Effective restrictions on commercial fishing, a stakeholder group with strong local representation, outsider funding support, and assistance from the tourism industry, especially Turneffe Flats Resort, have all helped turn local residents into supporters of the MPA.

One of the most successful marine protected areas is Cuba's Jardines de la Reina Marine Reserve, the largest MPA in the Caribbean. Daria Siciliano of The Ocean Foundation describes how this reserve, established in 1996, has helped protect a significant area of coral reefs from overfishing and other forms of destructive use. It now attracts nearly 1,000 divers every year, which is the limit established by managers, along with 500 catch-and-release fishers. Jardines de la Reina is one of over 100 MPAs in Cuba that collectively protect roughly one-third of the country's coral reefs, seagrass beds, and mangroves. As Siciliano points out, however, the combination of climate-induced change and American-driven tourism development could undermine the progress made by Cuban MPAs over the past few decades.

The final case study looks at the Cabo Pulmo National Park in Baja California Sur, Mexico. Martin Goebel and his co-authors look at the relationship between this important marine park and the nearby community of Cabo Pulmo, where local fishing families made the decision in the 1990s to embrace conservation and tourism to replace a declining fishing industry. As a result, Cabo Pulmo Reef has become one of the foremost diving sites in this part of the world, described by conservationist Dr. Sylvia Earle as the "jewel in the crown" of the Gulf of California. The price of this success, however, has been a rapid growth of tourism interest in the area, leading to development pressure that threatens the very resources on which tourism depends. This story has been repeated throughout the Caribbean and around the world.

Goals of this Volume

Our hope is that the essays and case studies in this volume do two things. First, they should clearly illustrate the perilous state of ocean ecosystems and resources as we enter the era of significant human-induced climate change. Even without rising temperatures, increased ocean acidity, and the other effects of global warming, many of these critical habitats and the fish and other species they support would already be under threat, mainly from human factors such as overfishing, pollution, and destructive forms of development. With the added stresses from climate change, crucial habitats like coral reefs, mangroves, and seagrass beds face a dire and uncertain future. Tourism has no doubt played a part in this unfortunate situation, especially in places like the Caribbean where visitors often outnumber local residents, use more resources, and have more impacts on the environment, including fragile marine ecosystems.

Secondly, and conversely, we hope that the case studies in particular show that tourism can play a more positive role with respect to climate change and the long-term survival of places like the Caribbean. From the coral reef nurseries of Puntacana to resort tourists eating locally sourced and sustainable seafood, the tourism industry can and must play a critical part in responding and adapting to the impacts of climate change, as well as other human-induced environmental impacts. Conservation measures like marine protected areas, especially when created with strong support from and involvement of local communities, can help ensure the protection of critical habitats like coral reefs, providing both food for local populations and income from the tourism activities that follow. These and other measures will be crucial to ensuring the futures of coastal communities in the Caribbean and beyond, many of which have come to depend as much or more on tourism as on traditional resources like fisheries. We hope, then, that the chapters in this volume provide as much room for optimism as they do fodder for despair as we face the uncertain, but clearly warmer, future that lies ahead.

CHAPTER 2

Coral Reefs and Marine Ecosystems in the Face of Climate Change

Overview—Coral Reef Decline in the Caribbean: Primary Causes and Implications for Management[1]

Rubén E. Torres and Jeremy Jackson

Caribbean coral reefs have suffered massive losses since the early 1980s due to a wide range of human impacts, including explosive human population growth, overfishing, coastal pollution, global warming, and invasive species. The consequences include widespread collapse of coral populations, increases in large seaweeds (macroalgae), outbreaks of coral bleaching and disease, and failure of corals to recover from natural disturbances such as hurricanes. Alarm bells were set off by a 2003 article in the journal *Science* that live coral cover on Caribbean reefs declined by roughly 80 percent from the 1970s to the early 2000s.[2] This dramatic decrease was closely followed by widespread and severe coral bleaching in 2005, which in turn was followed by high coral mortality due to disease at many reef locations.[3] Personal observations and multiple studies show that many Caribbean reefs today are like cleared forest, dominated by algae, with few if any large fish species and bearing little resemblance to their healthy past.[4]

Healthy corals are increasingly rare on the intensively studied reefs of the Florida reef tract, U.S. Virgin Islands, and Jamaica. Moreover, two of the formerly most abundant species, the elkhorn coral (*Acropora palmata*) and staghorn coral (*Acropora cervicornis*), have been added to the United States Endangered Species List. Concerns have mounted to the point that many NGOs have given up on Caribbean reefs and moved their attention elsewhere. It was against this gloomy backdrop that the current study was undertaken to rigorously assess the extent to which coral reef ecosystems throughout the wider Caribbean have declined, and for those that have not, to determine the factors responsible. Some reports, for example, have suggested that reefs in the southern Caribbean are in better ecological condition than elsewhere, with more live coral and reef fish.[5] Understanding why some reefs are healthier than others could provide an essential first step for more effective management to improve the condition of coral reefs throughout the entire Caribbean region.

There is a growing sense that reef degradation is inevitable as oceans continue to warm and waters become more acidic. Consequently, climate change dominates scientific and policy discussions to the virtual exclusion of everything else. What our study shows, however, is that other factors caused the decline of coral reefs even before widespread thermal changes in the Caribbean, and that these factors remain important today. Helping Caribbean coral reefs to survive the additional stress of climate change will require addressing these other factors, which may be more amenable to policy and management efforts.

The Caribbean Coral Reef Health Trends Study

To assess the state of coral reefs in the Caribbean and reasons for their decline, we conducted a detailed analysis of status and trends of reef communities at distinct locations throughout the Caribbean. We compiled essential metadata on the nature of the reef environment, depth, and history of human population growth, fishing, hurricanes, coral bleaching, and disease at each location. The specific biological information varied among locations, but wherever possible, data were obtained for coral and macroalgae cover, abundance of the critically important grazing sea urchin *Diadema antillarum*, and biomass of fishes, most importantly large grazing species.

Most quantitative data for Caribbean reefs are unpublished or buried in gray literature and government reports. To obtain these hard-to-find data, we contacted hundreds of researchers in all the countries of the Caribbean using several methods, including emails, requests posted on scientific websites, and in person at international conferences. We also corresponded with managers of all large reef monitoring programs in the region. In the end, we obtained data for corals, macroalgae, sea urchins, and fishes from more than 35,000 quantitative reef surveys from 1969 to 2012. This is the largest quantitative coral reef survey ever compiled, and exceeds by several times the amount of data used for earlier Caribbean assessments.

Data are distributed among 90 reef locations in 34 countries. Most are from fore-reef and patch-reef environments in depths between one and 20 meters, which are the focus of this study. Data for corals are extensive and range from 1970 to the present. Data for the formerly ubiquitous sea urchin, *Diadema antillarum,* are sparse until their mass mortality in 1983 to 1984, after which several monitoring programs began. Data for macroalgae are the most problematic because of inconsistent monitoring and taxonomy; therefore, much of those data had to be discarded from our analysis. Quantitative data for size and abundance of reef fishes, needed to estimate fish biomass, are unavailable until 1989 but extensive after that.

The longest time series from the same reefs are large photo quadrats from 1973 to the present for fixed sites at Curaçao and Bonaire, with newer time series from the same islands beginning in the 1990s. Comparable time series extending back to the early 1970s or 1980s are available for the northern Florida Keys, Jamaica, St. John and St. Croix in the U.S. Virgin Islands, and Panama. However, these records were compiled by different workers at different times and are therefore not as consistent or complete as data from the Dutch Caribbean.

The intensity of sampling varied greatly in time and space. We therefore partitioned the data into three time intervals of 12 to 14 years, each based on major ecological events that extended throughout the wider Caribbean. These are:

1. 1970 to 1983: From the oldest available data up to and including the mass mortality of the sea urchin *Diadema antillarum* in 1983;

also includes the first reports of White Band Disease (WBD) in the mid-1970s and early 1980s.

2. 1984 to 1998: From just after the *Diadema* die-off up to and including the 1998 extreme ocean warming event, with extensive global and regional coral bleaching and losses.

3. 1999 to 2011: The modern era of massively degraded coral reefs.

Current State of Caribbean Coral Reefs and Recent Trends

The current state of coral reefs in the Caribbean is poor. Our study shows that there has been a significant decline, on the order of 50 percent, in the extent of live coral on reefs throughout the region, with higher losses in some locations. Biodiversity, biomass, and important indicator species have all declined considerably in the time period studied, or roughly the past 45 years. Some species have become endangered or virtually extinct in that time. The full report provides a summary of the state of reefs throughout the Caribbean, with specific data on 34 countries.[6]

In terms of historical trends, the degradation of Caribbean reefs has apparently unfolded in three distinct phases:

Phase 1. Massive losses of *Acropora* corals from the mid-1970s to the early 1980s due to White Band Disease. These losses are unrelated to any obvious global environmental change and may have been due to introduced pathogens associated with enormous increases in ballast water discharge from bulk carrier shipping since the 1960s.

Phase 2. Very large increases in macroalgal cover and decreases in coral cover at most overfished locations following the 1983 mass mortality of *Diadema* (sea urchins), due to an unidentified and probably exotic pathogen. The shift in coral to macroalgal dominance reached a peak at most locations by the mid-1990s and has persisted throughout most of the Caribbean for 25 years. Numerous experiments show a link between macroalgal increase and coral decline. Macroalgae reduce coral recruitment and growth, are commonly toxic, and can induce coral disease.

Phase 3. From the late 1990s until today, there has been a continuation of patterns established in Phase 2, exacerbated by even greater overfishing, coastal pollution, explosions in tourism, and extreme warming events, often in combination. Die-offs have been particularly severe in the northeastern Caribbean and Florida Keys, where extreme bleaching followed by outbreaks of coral disease have caused the greatest declines.

Anthropogenic Causes of Coral Decline

According to our analysis, outbreaks of *Acropora* and *Diadema* diseases in the 1970s and early 1980s, overpopulation (including too many tourists), and overfishing are the three most important factors in the decline in Caribbean coral cover over the past 30 to 40 years. Coastal pollution is undoubtedly increasingly significant but there are too little data to tell. Increasingly warming seas pose an ominous threat, but so far extreme heating events have had only localized effects. Alone, they could not have been responsible for the great losses of Caribbean corals that occurred throughout most of the wider Caribbean region by the early to mid-1990s.

While disease outbreaks appear to be highly significant factors in the decline of coral in the Caribbean, they are perhaps the hardest to attribute directly to humans, and the hardest to control. We therefore focus in this section on four factors directly associated with human causes, and which therefore are the most logical areas in which to search for solutions.

1. Growth in Residents and Visitors

Tourism is the lifeblood of many Caribbean nations. However, the evidence shows that high densities of both tourists and residents are harmful to coral reefs unless environmental protections are comprehensive and effectively enforced. Unfortunately, this is rarely the case. Numbers of visitors per square kilometer per year ranged from a low of 110 in the Bahamas to an astounding 25,000 at St. Thomas. Tellingly, nearly all locations with more than 1,500 visitors per square kilometer per year have less than 14 percent coral cover. The only exception to this rule is Bermuda with 39 percent cover. The situation at Bermuda most likely reflects progressive environmental regulations in place since the 1990s, and the infrastructure required to make them work. Without such measures, the harmful environmental costs of runaway tourism, including their impacts on coral reefs, seem inevitable.

2. Overfishing

Artisanal fishing for subsistence is crucial to most Caribbean economies, but the consequences have been catastrophic for coral reefs. Overfishing has caused steep reductions in herbivores, especially large parrotfishes, which are the most effective grazers on Caribbean reefs and keep mac-roalgae and other coral competitors under control. The consequences for corals of overfishing parrotfish were little understood until the abrupt de-mise of sea urchins (*Diadema*) due to an unidentified disease in 1983 and 1984. Before then, *Diadema* had increasingly become the last important macroherbivore on Caribbean reefs, performing an ecological role previ-ously held by parrotfish and other large grazers. Reefs where parrotfishes had been overfished before 1984 suffered greater subsequent decreases in coral cover and increases in macroalgae than reefs that still had moder-ately intact populations of parrotfish.

Overfishing may also affect the capacity of reefs to recover from damage by storms, something they have done successfully for millions of years. Over the past few decades, corals have increasingly failed to become reestablished on many reefs after major storms. We investigated this apparent shift using data for 16 reefs with coral and *Diadema* data from before 1984. Coral cover was independent of the long-term probability of hurricanes before 1984, but not after. This suggests that overfishing of parrotfish, along with sea urchin decline, has decreased the ability of corals to recover after hurricanes. Recently overfished reefs on the Central Barrier in Belize, for example, declined by 49 percent after three hurricanes. Reefs protected from overfishing at Bermuda, meanwhile, experienced four hurricanes since 1984 with no loss in average coral cover.

3. Coastal Pollution and Water Quality

Comparative data for water transparency based on observations at three CARICOMP (Caribbean Coastal Marine Productivity Program, UNESCO) sites show that water quality is declining in areas of unregulated agricultural and coastal development. In particular, water transparency steeply declined over 20 years at Carrie Bow Cay in

Belize due to huge increases in agriculture and coastal development from Guatemala to Honduras. A similar pattern was observed at La Parguera on the west coast of Puerto Rico. In contrast, water quality improved in Bermuda, again thanks to stricter environmental policies and practices. Coral disease has been linked to excessive organic pollution but the data are spotty and limited in scope. There is a pressing need for more systematic and extensive monitoring of water quality throughout the wider Caribbean.

4. Ocean Warming

As a measure of ocean warming, we obtained data for degree heating weeks (DHWs) for all 88 localities in the study, with associated coral cover data from NOAA's Coral Reef Watch. We then used these data to assess the effects of the 1998, 2005, and 2010 extreme warming events on coral cover. Specifically, we calculated the change in coral cover for the 2 years following each event in relation to the 2 years before the event, and then plotted the proportional change in relation to the numbers of degree heating weeks (DHWs) experienced at each locality. There is a weak negative correlation between warming and changes in coral cover. Interestingly, the greatest losses in coral cover occurred at reef locations with fewer than 8 DHWs. Our results do not necessarily mean, however, that extreme heating events are unimportant drivers of coral mortality due to coral bleaching and disease, as they clearly have been in the U.S. Virgin Islands, Puerto Rico, Florida Keys, and elsewhere. Studies in the Virgin Islands, for example, suggest a complex relationship between extreme heating events, bleaching, and subsequent disease.[7] Increasingly frequent and severe extreme heating events will likely pose a greater threat to coral survival in future decades.

Conclusions and Implications for Management

Our findings stress the importance of bringing a historical perspective, as well as an extensive and comparative data set, to coral reef management and conservation discussions. Our results may contradict some recent rhetoric about the impacts of ocean warming on coral reefs, emphasizing instead the critical importance of other human factors such as increased population, coastal development, and overfishing. The threats of climate change and ocean acidification loom ominously for the future, but local stressors including an explosion in tourism, overfishing, and declines in water quality, along with resulting increases in macroalgae, have been the major drivers of the catastrophic decline of Caribbean corals in the recent past.

Smart decisions and actions at the local level can make an enormous difference for the well-being and resilience of Caribbean coral reefs and the people and enterprises that depend on them. Thus, four major recommendations emerged from our study that Caribbean nations and NGOs should take to heart:

1. Adopt robust conservation and fisheries management strategies that lead to restoration of parrotfish populations, including listing the parrotfish in relevant annexes of the Protocol Concerning Specially Protected Areas and Wildlife (SPAW protocol) of the UNEP Caribbean Environment Programme. A recommendation to this effect was passed unanimously at the October 2013 International Coral Reef Initiative Meeting in Belize.
2. Simplify and standardize monitoring of Caribbean reefs and make the results available on an annual basis to facilitate adaptive management.
3. Foster communication and exchange of information so that local authorities can benefit from the experiences of others elsewhere.
4. Develop and implement adaptive legislation and regulations to ensure that threats to coral reefs are systematically addressed, particularly threats posed by fisheries, tourism, and coastal development, as determined by established indicators of reef health.

We understand that action upon these recommendations will be a matter of local and national debate. But the implications of our scientific results are unmistakable: Caribbean coral reefs and their associated resources will virtually disappear within a few decades unless all of these measures are promptly adopted and enforced.

Notes

1. This essay is largely drawn from: Jeremy Jackson, Mary Dono-van, Katie Cramer and Vivian Lam, eds. (2014). Executive Summary. *Status and Trends of Caribbean Coral Reefs: 1970–2012*, Gland, Switzerland: Global Coral Reef Monitoring Network, International Union for the Conservation of Nature and Natural Resources. Available at: http://cmsdata.iucn.org/downloads/caribbean_coral_reefs___status_report_1970_2012.pdf. Use of material from the report is by permission of IUCN.

2. Toby Gardner, Isabelle Côté, Jennifer Gill, Alastair Grant, and Andrew Watkinson. (2003). Long-Term Region-Wide Declines in Caribbean Corals. *Science*, 301(5635), 958–960. Available at: http://www.jstor.org/stable/3834842.

3. Caroline Rogers, Erinn Muller, Tony Spitzack, and Jeff Miller. (2009). Extensive Coral Mortality in the US Virgin Islands in 2005/2006: A Review of the Evidence for Synergy Among Thermal Stress, Coral Bleaching and Disease. *Caribbean Journal of Science*, 45(2–3), 204–214. Available at: https://www.researchgate.net/profile/E_Muller/publication/258233179_Extensive_coral_mortality_in_the_US_Virgin_Islands_in_20052006_A_review_of_the_evidence_for_synergy_among_thermal_stress_coral_bleaching_and_disease/links/5409b8ac0cf2d8daaabe7bef.pdf.

4. Toby Gardner, et al. (2003). Op cit.

5. For example, see Jeremy Woodley, Kalli De Meyer, Philippe Bush, Gina Ebanks-Petrie, Jaime Garzon-Gerreira, Eduardo Klein, Leendert Pors, and Cornelius Wilson. (1997). Status of Coral Reefs in the South Central Caribbean. *Proceedings of the 8th International Coral Reef Symposium, Vol. 1,* 357–362. Panama City: Smithsonian Tropical Research Institute.

6. Jeremy Jackson, et al. eds. (2014). Op cit.

7. Caroline Rogers, et al. (2009). Op cit.

Case Study 2.1

The Puntacana Coral Gardens Program: Climate Change, Coral Reef Restoration, and Education

by Victor M. Galvan and Jake Kheel

The Puntacana Coral Gardens Program in the Dominican Republic was started in 2004 as a pilot project under a collaborative agreement between the Grupo Puntacana Foundation (GPCF) and Counterpart International (CPI). The program, also developed in collaboration with the University of Miami's Rosenstiel School of Marine and Atmospheric Science, uses coral transplantation as an active, hands-on tool that involves multiple stakeholder groups in coral reef conservation and restoration.[1] GPCF, which became involved in the project as part of its Partnership for Ecologically Sustainable Coastal Areas (PESCA) program, aimed to use coral reef restoration as a tool for biodiversity conservation, to improve the livelihoods of local residents including those involved in the tourism sector, and to increase the resilience of local coral reefs to mediate future impacts of climate change.

The Puntacana Coral Gardens Program focuses on preventing the threatened staghorn coral (*Acropora cervicornis*) from possible national or regional extinction through the establishment of coral nurseries where the few remaining wild genotypes can be rescued and multiplied in a protected setting. Vollmer and Kline[2] have shown that as many as 6 percent of staghorn genotypes are resistant to white band disease, identified as a leading cause for the decline of this species (along with other stressors like increased hurricane activity, overabundance of coral predators, and warming ocean temperatures). Resistant genotypes, which have apparently survived multiple exposures to extreme temperature and disease outbreaks, can potentially be crossed to create stronger offspring that are more resilient to future effects of climate change. Small, fast growing, and genetically diverse nursery-reared fragments can then be transplanted back onto degraded reefs to encourage natural recovery of the species.[3]

The location for the Coral Gardens Program is the Puntacana Resort and Club (PCRC), Punta Cana, Dominican Republic.[4] PCRC and GPCF are engaged in a number of projects designed to attract tourists interested in environmental sustainability and resource conservation.[5] The Coral Gardens Program is a feature that attracts green-minded tourists, especially recreational divers and others interested in coral reef health and conservation.[6] Reef restoration efforts using nursery transplants have taken place throughout the entire PCRC reef area and the newly formed Punta Cana Marine Protected Area for Habitat and Species (Presidential Decree 356-12). Staghorn corals have become very rare in the area; in recent years only a handful of wild colonies have been found, and these were in a state of decline. The objective of the project is to multiply the few remaining *Acropora* genotypes in a nursery setting using different types of platforms to produce a continuous, genetically diverse and reliable source of fragments for restoration efforts.

Nursery Location and Design

The Puntacana coral nursery, the largest such facility in the Dominican Republic, is located at the very popular Aquarium dive site. The nursery is located at depths ranging from 3 to 10 meters and surrounded by shallow reef. The reef forms an irregular perimeter around the sand flat, reducing wave action and making the nursery accessible under most weather conditions. The site contains two natural sea passages that allow for excellent water circulation. Water temperatures monitored between February 2010 and October 2011 ranged from 25° to 29° Celsius, only exceeding 30° C a couple of times in late summer.

In terms of coral production, one A-frame was set up in 2005 with roughly 7 meters of tissue from six different genotypes. As of 2013, the nursery contained 31 growth platforms including three fix-to-bottom tables (Image 2.1.1), one midwater nursery (Image 2.1.2), and 27 metal A-frames (Image 2.1.3). These structures contained an estimated 1,902 fragments totaling roughly 1,665 meters of staghorn tissue, with 12 genotypes being tracked. Four pillar coral (*Dendrogyra cyclindrus*) fragments have also been rescued and added to the nursery.

The Aquarium dive site, home to the coral nursery, is now one of the most visited marine sites in Punta Cana. The biological life at the coral nursery, and its proximity to tour operators, make this site ideal for educational and recreational purposes. To help protect the site, mooring buoys were installed to eliminate the use of anchors, while underwater signage and rope routes were installed to reduce physical damage from divers. In addition, an informal agreement with local fishermen prohibits fishing within the Aquarium. These actions have led to increased coral cover in this zone when compared to other areas in Punta Cana, and a fish biomass deemed to be among the highest in the Caribbean.

Since 2010, the project has expanded from 2 to 13 coral nurseries throughout the Dominican Republic, with nurseries now present in almost all tourism hotspots. Nurseries have been established using local volunteers and knowledge. Transfer-of-knowledge requests have also been received from institutions representing at least 5 Caribbean nations, including Haiti. We believe the lessons from the Puntacana Coral Gardens Program can be applied to help restore coral reefs throughout the Caribbean and to link these important efforts to the tourism and diving industries, thereby increasing public awareness of coral reef threats and conservation.

Image 2.1.1 *Fix-to-bottom table used for propagating genotypes with limited tissue; increased growth and decreased predation are frequently observed* [7]

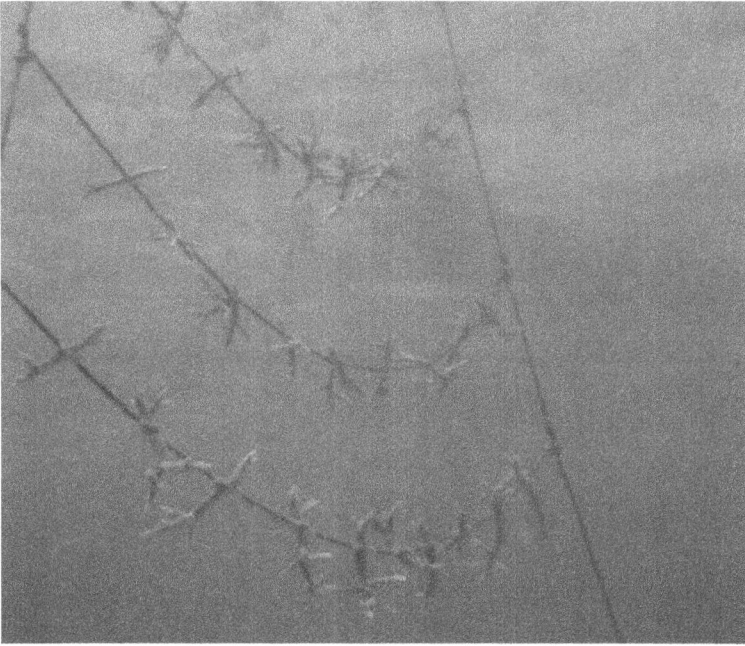

Image 2.1.2 Midwater nursery with horizontal lines connected to two vertical ropes anchored to the bottom and suspended by buoys

Images 2.1.3 Metal A-frame features resin-coated metal mesh anchored to the bottom with rebar and cable ties

Transplant Sites and Methods

Multiple coral transplant sites have been set up with the assistance of local certified fishermen and interns. Transplant sites are located close to shore at depths of 2 to 11 meters, similar to nursery depths. Site selection is based on criteria established by The Nature Conservancy and their partners, including NOAA, Counterpart International, and the University of Miami.[8] Experimental transplant sites roughly 400 meters apart are first set up with at least three genotypes each. These are monitored regularly and high-performing sites are expanded. Galvanized masonry nails and cable ties are used to transplant larger fragments. Smaller fragments

Images 2.1.4, 2.1.5, and 2.1.6 Transplant efforts at PCRC include cementing staghorn colonies onto natural reefs (above); establishing new transplant sites using the nail and cable tie method (next page, top); and nailing a frame filled with small fragments that have formed a thicket onto a denuded reef (next page, bottom)[9]

Images 2.1.4, 2.1.5, and 2.1.6 (Continued)

are encrusted into holes in the reef. Transplanted fragment sizes average 59 cm (range of 41 to 84 cm) at Punta Cana.

A total of 46 transplant sites and 27 expansions have been established since 2012, with 32 sites and 19 expansions created in 2014 alone. As of 2014, a total of 5,277 staghorn colonies with more than 2.7 km of nursery-reared tissue have been restored onto natural reefs with an average mortality rate of just 8.2 percent (range of 0 to 28.7 percent, N = 19).

Nursery Maintenance and Operation

The Grupo Puntacana Foundation, with support from its PESCA project partners, developed the PADI Coral First Aid Specialty Course[10] to teach divers about the ecology and conservation of coral reefs. As of 2015, ten local fishermen had been certified in SCUBA and Coral Reef Conservation by PADI. Two of these fishermen were hired as coral gardeners to perform nursery maintenance such as removing algae, replacing damaged nursery structures, and removing dead coral fragments (which helps eliminate hiding places for predators and reduces drag and weight, prolonging the life of the nursery structures). One fisherman was hired to be the project's boat captain and act as liaison between GPCF and local fishermen.

Several local fishermen's associations have also been established. The association in Punta Cana includes three female artisans and three male coral gardeners. The artisans are helping GPCF control the invasive lionfish population[11] by creating taxidermied lionfish products sold through various partners. Association members are also being trained as presenters and guides for the new tourism circuits being developed.

To help train young professionals, a highly competitive six-month internship program was created that attracts more than 50 national and international applicants each year. Interns help manage the coral nursery program, including assisting with environmental education, disease eradication, and predator control activities. Over a dozen interns have become employees of the program or been hired elsewhere, including two young fishermen now running coral nurseries in Haiti and the north coast of the Dominican Republic.

In addition to fishers, some 11 dive instructors, 10 Dominican science students, and several international tourists have been certified in coral gardening. Actively involving tourists can help program sustainability, while having coral nurseries at tourism destinations shows visitors that hotels and resorts are interested in preserving the natural resources of the area. This can attract visitors seeking more environmentally responsible destinations and can result in increased loyalty to a destination. In addition to diving at nursery sites, excursions revolving around coral transplantation efforts have been developed to attract new customers to the resorts and generate funds to continue these programs.

Lessons Learned

We have learned a number of lessons that could benefit those considering similar projects. First, do not begin coral gardens or nurseries as a public relations gimmick or fundraising tool. Coral restoration requires an ongoing budget for maintenance and outplanting. In the Dominican Republic, some local foundations have promoted coral gardens as a means to attract private donations from companies or to get media attention. Often, these nurseries are not maintained and there are no plans or resources to perform any outplanting. It is relatively easy to build a nursery of corals on frame. The real work of maintaining them, transplanting coral fragments, and conducting research on survival rates requires a commitment over time and dedicated resources. Creating ghost nurseries is a poor use of resources.

Second, we recommend diversifying nursery infrastructure to reduce the chances of total loss due to storms and thermal stress, both of which are increased by climate change. Almost all materials used (nails, cable ties, rebar, etc.) can be found locally, and structures should be made as inexpensively as possible to allow low-income coastal communities to participate. The nail and cable tie transplantation method can be time consuming, but has resulted in good coral retention in high energy areas and allows for very large coral colonies to be transplanted using multiple attachment points.

Third, nursery size and the rate of expansion should be based on the resources available. A nursery that expands too fast can outpace maintenance and transplantation efforts, leading to over-mature corals and the selection of poorer transplant sites just to get tissue out. One of the biggest problems in our nurseries is too much tissue and not enough outplanting back onto the reef. This means that nurseries can always be threatened by storm events or other catastrophic impacts and their coral stocks could be completely lost.

Fourth, evaluate nursery infrastructure needs and types. Some nursery platforms can serve as refuges from extreme temperature events[12] and can be easily adjusted during high temperatures when coral growth is slower. Monitor, identify, and promote natural sexual reproduction of temperature- and disease-resistant genotypes to build resilience. Climate change impacts can influence survivorship, as stress from high temperatures is one likely cause for increased initial mortality of transplanted coral.[13]

Finally, fragment size at transplantation is important; larger coral pieces can reduce mortality from predation, smothering, and competition, and can increase rates of growth.[14] Typically, more branches mean greater growth potential. Smaller fragments, however, can be wedged onto reefs and may be appropriate for some locations. To reduce losses from predation, deploy predator traps before and during transplantation. Target protected areas with remnant staghorn colonies, and avoid areas of high sedimentation and *Agaricia* (stony corals).

Conclusions

We have shown over the last 10 years that coral conservation and restoration is an efficient tool that, when combined with other resource management practices, can be beneficial for local communities, the scientific community, and the tourism industry. Our coral restoration efforts, supported by volunteers, interns, and tourists in Punta Cana, have seen an incredible amount of coral tissue returned to local reefs, above and beyond natural population levels. This has allowed us to contribute to the preservation and conservation of staghorn coral, one of the first coral species listed for protection under the U.S. Endangered Species Act.

Further, through these restoration efforts we have been able to build trust and forge collaborative agreements with local fishing communities, allowing the Puntacana Resort and Club to establish a no-fishing zone where fish populations have rebounded and coral cover continues to increase. This zone has become one of the primary tourism attractions in the area and is a prime example of how conservation efforts can be combined with recreational activities to be economically productive.

Over the 10 years of the Puntacana Coral Gardens Program, we have shown that conservation and tourism can benefit each other and have developed ideas for alternative income generation activities that can benefit the local fishing community. We have shared here these successes as well as some challenges and difficulties we have encountered. In so doing, we hope to make this program replicable by other institutions that share the mission and vision of the Grupo Puntacana Foundation, including helping coral reefs, the communities that depend on them, and the tourism industry they support survive and thrive in the face of climate change.

Acknowledgment of Project Partners and Financial Support

The Puntacana Coral Gardens Program was established by the director of Corals for Conservation, Dr. Austin Bowden-Kerby, with financial support from Counterpart International (CPI). The program was brought to scale with the help of Dr. Diego Lirman at the University of Miami's Rosenstiel School of Marine and Atmospheric Science. Financial assistance was also provided by Grupo Puntacana Foundation, Counterpart International, and the Frohring Foundation. Additional support was provided by the Small Grants Program from the United Nations Environment Program, project number DOM/SPG/OP5/CORE/BD/2012/18; an Inter-American Development Bank technical collaboration, number ATN /ME:13126-DR; the Starwood Foundation; and the Punta Cana Airport Sun and Fun Charity Golf Tournament.

Notes

1. Punta Cana Resort and Club. (2015). *Coral Gardens Represent an Innovative Way to Conserve Endangered Coral Species.* Available at: http://www.puntacana.org/coral/index.html.

2. Steven Vollmer and David Kline. (2008). Natural Disease Resistance in Threatened Staghorn Corals. *PLoS One,* 3(11), e3718. Available at: http://journals.plos.org/plosone/article?id=10.1371/journal.pone.0003718.

3. Austin Bowden-Kerby. (2013). *Coral First Aid: PADI Distinctive Specialty: Training Manual for SCUBA Divers.* Available at: https://www .padi.com/padi-courses/project-aware-coral-reef-conservation-course.

4. Punta Cana is the geographical location, while Puntacana is the spelling used by the resort.

5. Stephen Uzzo. (2013). Puntacana Ecological Foundation and the Scaling of Sustainable Tourism Development. *Ecology and Society,* 18(4), 73. Available at: http://dx.doi.org/10.5751/ES-06259-180473.

6. Anonymous. (2013). Environmentalists Eye Coral Gardens as the Next Big Tourist Attraction. *Dominican Today,* November 7, 2013. Available at: http://www.dominicantoday.com/dr/business-and -pleasure/2013/11/7/49562/Environmentalists-eye-coral-gardens -as-the-next-big-tourist-attraction.

7. Source of Images 2.1.1 to 2.1.3: Guillermo Ricart; Victor Galvan.

8. Meaghan E. Johnson, Caitlin Lustic, Erich Bartels, Iliana B. Baums, David S. Gilliam, Liz Larson, Diego Lirman, Margaret W. Miller, Ken Nedimyer, and Stephanie Schopmeyer. (2011). *Caribbean Acropora Restoration Guide: Best Practices for Propagation and Population Enhancement.* Arlington, Virginia: The Nature Conservancy. Available at: http://www.reefresilience.org/pdf/Johnson_etal_2011 _Acropora-Coral-Guide.pdf.

9. Source of Images 2.1.4 to 2.1.6: Brianna Bambic, Morgan Hightshoe, and Victor Galvan.

10. PADI, the Professional Association of Diving Instructors, offers training and certification in areas such as rescue, first aid and open water diving. For information on coral reef conservation certification see https://www.padi.com/scuba-diving/padi-courses/course-catalog/aware-%E2%80%93-coral-reef-conservation-course/.

11. Originally from the Indo-Pacific, the lionfish (*Pterois miles y P. Volitans*) was introduced to the Caribbean as a result of the commercial aquarium trade. In 2008, lionfish began to populate the reefs of the Dominican Republic. The species has the capacity to do great damage to reefs for a variety of reasons, including decimating native fish species. GPCF began its Lionfish Control Program in 2011 through the use of this invasive (but highly edible) species in the restaurants of Puntacana Resort & Club, as well as through a lionfish taxidermy program, which provides revenue for local artisans.

12. Stephanie Schopmeyer, Diego Lirman, Erich Bartels, James Byrne, David Gilliam, John Hunt, Meaghan Johnson, Elizabeth Larson, Kerry Maxwell, Ken Nedimyer, and Cory Walter. (2011). *In-Situ* Coral Nurseries Serve as Genetic Repositories for Coral Reef Restoration After an Extreme Cold-Water Event. *Restoration Ecology,* 20(6), 696–703.

13. James Herlan and Diego Lirman. (2008). Development of a Coral Nursery Program for the Threatened Coral *Acropora Cervicornis* in Florida. In: *Proceedings from the 11th International Coral Reef Symposium, Vol. 2,* 1249–1255. Ft. Lauderdale, Florida: ReefBase. Available at: http://www.reefbase.org/resource_center/publication/pub_27703.aspx.

14. James Herlan and Diego Lirman. (2008). Op cit.

Case Study 2.2

Mangrove Restoration and Community Co-Management in Telescope, Grenada

by Dieter Rothenberger and Aria St. Louis[1]

Background

As a small island in the southeastern Caribbean Sea, Grenada is particularly vulnerable to the adverse effects of climate change. Extreme events such as hurricanes are likely to become more intense in the future. Two prolonged dry spells with devastating consequences to the agriculture sector occurred in the past 5 years. According to studies, as little as a 0.5 m (1.5 ft.) sea level rise (SLR) could cause severe erosion at the world famous, picture perfect Grand Anse Beach, causing up to 75 percent of the beach to disappear.[2] A similar SLR could virtually eliminate other major beaches including Marquis Beach and Soubise Beach.[3]

Most Grenadians live in low-lying coastal areas vulnerable to many negative impacts of climate change. Most development and infrastructure in the tri-island state is concentrated along the coast, including airports, major roads, cities and towns, hotels, marinas, fishing villages, and valuable agricultural land. Grenada's coastal zone is a vital but increasingly vulnerable area, needing sound management to properly adapt to anticipated impacts of a changing climate.

To address these issues, Grenada and Germany jointly launched the pilot program Integrated Climate Change Adaptation Strategies (ICCAS), which places one focus on how coastal zones and their respective ecosystems in Grenada are managed. The ICCAS program is funded by the German Federal Ministry for the Environment, Nature Conservation, Building and Nuclear Safety (BMUB) under its International Climate Initiative (IKI). The program is implemented in Grenada by the Environment Division, Ministry of Agriculture, Lands, Forestry, Fisheries and Environment (MALFFE) of the Government of Grenada; the Deutsche Gesellschaft für Internationale Zusammenarbeit[4] (GIZ); and the United Nations Development Programme (UNDP).

To support Grenada in a robust and integrated manner, ICCAS uses a multilevel approach to institutional and technical capacity development. On the national level, a Coastal Zone Policy[5] has been developed and approved by Cabinet, and a Coastal Zone Task Force institutionalized with the support of more than 10 different authorities, ministerial departments, and other institutions. At the sectoral level, intense capacity building has taken place with regard to climate-sensitive tourism. In collaboration with the Center for Responsible Travel (CREST) in the United States and the Grenada Hotel and Tourism Authority (GHTA), more than 40 representatives from the tourism sector were exposed to key information on how the tourism sector can help make Grenada's coast more climate resilient. Finally, on the community level, GIZ and the Forestry and National Parks Department (FNPD), jointly with the Environment Division of MALFFE, are implementing a project called Restoration and Community Co-Management of Mangroves (RECCOMM) to strengthen the resilience of mangrove and coastal ecosystems and create sustainable livelihoods for the community.

The RECCOMM Project

The objective of the RECCOMM pilot project is to increase the health of the mangrove forest and associated ecosystems and reduce vulnerabilities to the adverse impacts of climate change. The project is multidisciplinary and takes input from various institutional, nongovernmental,

Image 2.2.1 The coastal area of Telescope is subject to heavy erosion by wave action paired with poor environmental practices[6]

and community stakeholders. The project site is located in Telescope in St. Andrew, Grenada. The coastal communities in the project area are highly vulnerable to the adverse effects of climate change such as storm surges and sea level rise. They are also some of the most impoverished communities on the island. The project area is experiencing heavy coastal erosion partially due to past sand mining activities. Additionally, the mangroves that act as the first natural line of defense are being reduced by deforestation and unsustainable harvesting practices to produce charcoal.

Findings of Baseline Study

An extensive baseline study of the project area has been completed.[7] Data collected included beach profiling, mapping of mangrove trees and other species in the project area, soil sampling, and conducting a socioeconomic analysis using interviews and focus group discussions. A survey showed that 93 percent of respondents had observed changes in the beach and landscape. These changes included coastal erosion (identified by 56 percent of respondents), loss of vegetation (19 percent), and encroaching seas (14 percent). Respondents believed that the majority of these changes were the result of sand mining activities, deforestation for residential and farming purposes, and ongoing production of charcoal. To reverse these changes the majority (51 percent) of respondents suggested replanting mangroves and other coastal vegetation. Another 14 percent suggested increased enforcement of sand mining laws and improved mangrove protection.

Based on these findings, the following key recommendations have been developed:

- Carefully select species for replanting, including white mangrove, black mangrove, red mangrove, buttonwood mangrove, sea grape, almond, seaside mahoe, and coconut. In response to predicted sea level rise, red mangrove should be considered to increase the resilience of mangrove areas against saltwater inflows.
- A capacity building program on the importance of sustainable management of forests is needed to address behaviors and practices that contribute to the environmental problems observed in the project area.
- The Forestry Department should supervise harvesting of mangroves for charcoal production to ensure that removal of branches, stems,

and suckers does not adversely affect ecological, recreational, and environmental functions. *Leucaena leucocephala* and *Acacia mangium* were recommended for woodlots for charcoal production because they are fast growing, have high heating values, and are tolerant to salt and low pH conditions.

- Further strengthen the capacity of the Telescope community for self-reliance, climate change mitigation and adaptation, and environmental sustainability.

Project Implementation

Based on these recommendations, the RECCOMM project in Telescope included four technical components:

1. Replanting of mangroves.
2. Sustainable mangrove harvesting, including planting alternative species.
3. Introduction of beekeeping as an alternative livelihood.
4. Use of mangrove areas and adjacent lake as an ecotourism site.

To build institutional capacity and support implementation, a co-management structure, the Northern Telescope Mangrove Management Board (NTMMB), was established. This helps the community work with government officials to manage the project, and also helps to enforce mangrove protection policies in Telescope. Community ownership of the project is ensured, while limited government staff resources are supplemented, supporting long-term protection of the mangroves. It is hoped that if successful, the project can be expanded to other locations with similar ecosystems and social structures.

Project Achievements

To date, the following steps have been accomplished:

- The Northern Telescope Mangrove Management Board (NTMMB) has been established. It is comprised of five members from the local community and one from the St. Andrew Development Organization (SADO), as well as members from the Ministry of Tourism and Culture and four Divisions of the MALFFE (Forestry, Fisheries, Apiculture and the Environment). Monthly board meetings have been held.

- The community members of the NTMMB have received training regarding operation of a community-based organization as a step toward formal registration.
- Community consultations were held to inform and involve the community in the project. These meetings saw thorough discussions and resulted in high interest in the mangrove replanting and protection components, and in sustainable livelihoods components such as beekeeping, sustainable charcoal management, and ecotourism.
- Local charcoal producers have been identified and made aware of the project through meetings. Signs explaining the mangrove protection project have been installed at strategic access points to the mangroves.
- Around 20 community members took part in an introductory beekeeping course and an intensive three-day workshop at the Caribbean Bee College at St. George's University. A three-month beekeeping course by a trainer from MALFFE, held at the T.A. Marryshow Community College in Mirabeau, provided participants with skills needed to operate as professional beekeepers. Participants are currently creating a local beekeepers' cooperative.
- Beehives were placed close to the project site with the mangroves and nearby agricultural lands providing excellent foraging sources

Image 2.2.2 Participants in an intensive beekeeping course learn how to manage hives and collect honey for additional income[8]

for the bees. This adds value to the mangroves and contributes to their sustainable use.

- Over 1,200 mangrove seedlings were planted at the project site between November 2015 and February 2016. These plants are continuously monitored by members of the community, who track

Image 2.2.3 *Mangrove seedlings that were allowed to grow over a few weeks are now ready to be planted*[9]

Image 2.2.4 *Planting of mangrove seedlings by a Telescope community member*[10]

growth patterns and note changes in the features and numbers of the plants. The planted areas have been fenced to improve their visibility to users of the mangrove. Along with the mangrove seedlings, other species such as neem, almond, and sea grape were planted.

- Awareness activities were conducted during mangrove planting, and an educational fun fair held at the community playing field, to inform the broader public about the project.

Next Steps

The next phase in the project will help reinforce its environmental goals and bring greater economic sustainability to local residents. Planned steps include:

- A boardwalk will be installed through the mangroves with interpretation signs about their importance as ecosystems and explaining different mangrove species. A bird hide (blind) will be placed at the end to enable birdwatching and wildlife observation. This will help maintain the ecosystem's integrity and provide opportunities to experience local birds, animals, flora, and the seascape.

- An ecotourism training manual is being developed in cooperation with the Ministry of Tourism. The manual will be used to help train community members to act as local ecotourism guides. In addition, an existing building of the Grenada Solid Waste Management Authority will be used as an information venue for ecotourists, including providing drinks and snacks to generate additional local income.

- A training and capacity building program in sustainable charcoal production will be implemented for local charcoal producers. In addition, alternative fast-growing species of trees will be planted to help transition charcoal makers away from mangrove species.

- The NTMMB will be established as a formal co-management mechanism to support enforcement of mangrove and ecosystem protection regulations. Board members will be trained on their roles and responsibilities in the future.

- Continuing efforts will be made to increase community awareness about the importance of mangroves as interconnected ecosystems with multiple benefits, and as a natural coastal defense against rising sea levels and beach erosion.

Notes

1. Written with assistance and contributions by Andre Joseph-Witzig, Technical Officer, Environment Division, MALFFE, and Maxine Welsh, Technical Officer, GIZ-ICCAS Project.
2. Rawleston Moore and Leon Charles, eds. (2014). *Grenada's Coastal Vulnerability and Risk Assessment.* CPACC Component 6 Report (Technical Report 5C/CPACC-02-01-3). Belmopan, Belize: Caribbean Community Climate Change Centre. Available at: http://dms.caribbeanclimate.bz/M-Files/openfile.aspx?objtype=0&docid=5722.
3. M.C. Simpson, J.F. Clarke, D.J. Scott, M. New, A. Karmalkar, O.J. Day, M. Taylor, S. Gossling, M. Wilson, D. Chadee, H. Stager, R. Waithe, A. Stewart, J. Georges, N. Hutchinson, N. Fields, R. Sim, M. Rutty, L. Matthews, S. Charles and A. Agosta G'meiner. (2012). *CARIBSAVE Climate Change Risk Atlas (CCCRA)–Grenada.* Barbados: DFID, AusAID and The CARIBSAVE Partnership.
4. As a federal enterprise, GIZ supports the Government of Germany in achieving its objectives in the field of international cooperation for sustainable development.
5. Ministry of Agriculture, Lands, Forestry, Fisheries and the Environment of the Government of Grenada (MALFFE). (2015). *Integrated Coastal Zone Policy for Grenada, Carriacou and Petite Martinique.* St. Georges: MALFEE. Policy paper submitted to the Cabinet of Ministers in Grenada, prepared with support from the GIZ-ICCAS program and the regional Caribbean Aqua-Terrestrial Solutions (CATS) programme, which is implemented by GIZ and CARICOM on behalf of the German Federal Ministry for Economic Cooperation and Development (BMZ).
6. Image Source: Andre Joseph Witzig, MALFFE.
7. Deutsche Gesellschaft für Internationale Zusammenarbeit (GIZ). (2014). *Strengthening Telescope Mangrove and Coastal Resilience for Climate Change Adaptation and Sustainable Livelihoods – A Project Baseline Study.* St. Georges: Grenada Fund for Conservation (GFC).
8. Image Source: Andre-Joseph Witzig, MALFFE.
9. Image Source: Maxine Welsh, GIZ-ICCAS.
10. Image Source: Maxine Welsh, GIZ-ICCAS.

Case Study 2.3

Strangled by Seaweed:
The *Sargassum* Invasion in Mexico and the Caribbean

by Jake Kheel and Kreg Ettenger

While coral reefs, mangroves, and seagrasses in the Caribbean and world-wide are being lost to climate change and other human-induced forces, other components of marine ecosystems are apparently on the upswing. One in particular, sargassum seaweed, has recently become a threat to the Caribbean, appearing in new places and in record amounts. Far from being a welcome arrival, however, sargassum is wreaking havoc with coastal and marine habitats and impacting the region's tourism economy. While the exact source of the seaweed and the reasons for its rapid rise are still unclear, many suspect that warming ocean temperatures, an increase in the amount of nutrients in coastal areas, and changing ocean currents all play some part.

Emergence of the Problem

In the summer of 2011, large wracks of sargassum[1] began to drift into the Caribbean, landing with much fanfare on its beaches in amounts never before seen. The *New York Times* documented this mysterious and un-precedented invasion in October of 2011, describing the impact it was having on resorts and coastal communities that depend on tourism.[2] "Though not a threat to human health," the article stated, "the seaweed, which attracts flies and smells like rotten eggs as it decomposes, is a nuisance at best and a repellent at worst."

Given the lack of historical data on such invasions, the article offered little clarity as to whether this was an exceptional event or represented a regime shift, possibly due to changes in ocean currents or other factors. Abnormally large sargassum landings continued in the Caribbean through 2012, then declined, only to resume in 2014 and 2015. In the summer of 2015, researchers tracking sargassum by satellite described the coverage in the Caribbean and eastern Mexico as the largest in history.

Image 2.3.1 A thick layer of sargassum covers a beach in Barbados. The huge wracks of seaweed can harm wildlife including nesting turtles and can make beaches virtually unusable for tourism, or require expensive cleanup operations[3]

Chuanmin Hu, a University of South Florida professor, calculated there was over 12,000 sq. mi. (31,000 km^2) of sargassum in the Caribbean, an area larger than Haiti and nearly five times the amount recorded in 2011. And in February of 2016, based on pilots' observations and other data, the St. Maarten Nature Foundation warned that 2016 levels of sargassum could rival those of earlier outbreaks.[4]

Some experts are convinced that the once sporadic landings of sargassum have become the new normal in the Caribbean and Gulf of Mexico. Meetings and conferences have been held to discuss the problem and look for solutions. Research dollars are being dedicated to understanding the reasons for this new scourge, and millions are being spent on beach cleanup in the region. At an August 2015 symposium, Vice Chancellor of the University of the West Indies (UWI) Sir Hilary Beckles called sargassum "the greatest single threat to the Caribbean tourism industry" and proposed an international Sargassum Emergency Agency to deal with the economic and ecological crisis.[5]

The region's tourism industry has already suffered from lost reservations and bad reviews. Negative publicity has come from multiple sources, including stories in the *Washington Post*,[6] *New York Magazine*,[7] and *Smithsonian*.[8] Even normally upbeat industry sources like *Travel Weekly*[9] and *Travel Agent Central*[10] have sounded the alarm. And consumer travel review sites like TripAdvisor have been awash with negative reviews as visitors have been surprised and sometimes horrified by unswimmable beaches and mountainous piles of stinking, decaying seaweed. Website postings in 2015 and 2016 indicated that sargassum was a problem on mainland beaches from Texas to the Yucatán peninsula to the Dominican Republic, and on many Caribbean islands as well.

In addition to serious impacts on local and regional tourism, the masses of seaweed threaten coastal ecosystems as well as the livelihoods of local fishing communities. Sea turtles can find nesting areas blocked by dense piles of sargassum, while hatchlings are sometimes unable to reach the water due to the seaweed, which can reach several meters in height. Fish can become entangled or have to move out of choked bays and other areas, where decomposing seaweed can deprive waters of oxygen. And the lack of sunlight under floating mats of seaweed can affect seagrasses and other plants, as well as the multiple species that depend on them.

Possible Causes for Invasion

Theories explaining the explosion of sargassum are almost as abundant as the seaweed itself. According to different sources, landings may be due to global climate change, shifting or slowing ocean currents, El Niño weather events, Saharan dust clouds, nutrients from Brazilian Amazon farms, and even dispersants used during the British Petroleum Deepwater Horizon oil spill. It is still too early, however, to say definitively what is causing the recent explosion in sargassum on Caribbean beaches, and a combination of factors might be at play.

Sargassum is actually a unique and fascinating floating habitat that has enormous economic, ecological, and even climatic benefits. The Sargasso Sea, where most Atlantic sargassum is normally found, is a vast area with large floating mats of sargassum (as well as, increasingly, plastics) defined by ocean currents rather than by land boundaries. At two million square miles, it is roughly the size of the United States. Recognizing its importance as a marine ecosystem, the Sargasso Sea Commission was formed in 2014 to protect the vital habitat and develop conservation management strategies to minimize human impacts on it.[11]

The Sargasso Sea is immensely productive, serving as home and spawning area to at least 10 endemic species (found only in the floating masses of sargassum), plus 145 invertebrates and 127 fish species. Sargassum provides important nurseries, shelters, and feeding stations for numerous endangered and/or commercially important species, including wahoo, tuna, sharks, sperm and humpback whales, sea turtles, and numerous migratory birds. Endangered American eels and flying fish both use sargassum for part of their life cycles. The Sargasso Sea is also suspected of being an important player in the global ocean sequestration (natural storage) of carbon. Sargassum is a strong net carbon sink that helps the oceans absorb carbon dioxide and thereby regulate global climate. As climate change accelerates, this type of sink could become increasingly important.

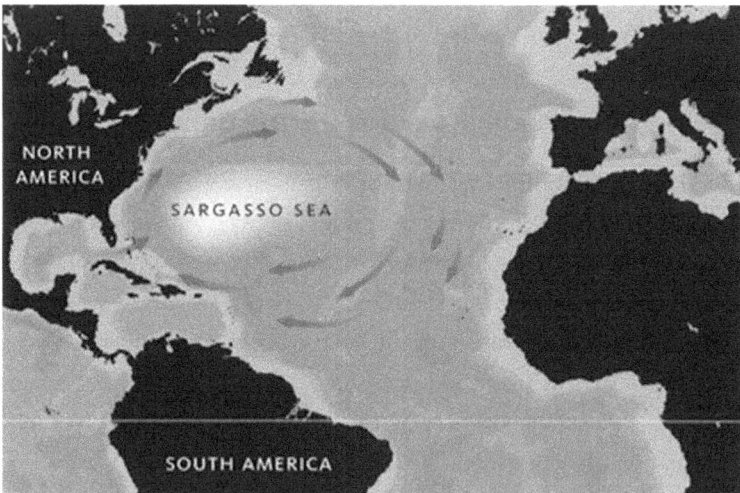

Image 2.3.2 One suggested source for the sargassum that has recently plagued Caribbean beaches is the Sargasso Sea, where masses of the floating seaweed normally reside. Changing ocean temperatures may be affecting Atlantic currents, allowing more of the sargassum to enter and remain in the Caribbean, according to some scientists[12]

The two species of sargassum most commonly found in the Sargasso Sea (*S. fluitans* and *S. natans)* are *holopelagic*, meaning they reproduce on the high seas, as opposed to other seaweed species that start their life cycles at the bottom of the ocean. Sargassum feeds on nutrients in the water column and forms massive floating rafts of seaweed that are moved about by ocean currents. This unique mobility and capacity to expand while on the move provides a distinct clue as to why sargassum has become such a problem in the Caribbean.

Some scientists believe that a weakening of the Gulf Stream and other Atlantic currents might be allowing sargassum from the Sargasso Sea to be pushed into the Caribbean and the Gulf of Mexico rather than be carried northward and swept into the Atlantic gyre. Sargassum that grows naturally in the Gulf of Mexico and Caribbean Sea, meanwhile, is not getting pulled out of these waters and into the Atlantic. Even more recent research suggests that the type of sargassum now plaguing Caribbean beaches, dubbed *S. natans VIII Parr*, does not originate in the Sargasso Sea at all but in a region farther south called the North Equatorial Recirculation Region. This area, which lies between eastern South America and western Africa, might also be experiencing changes in currents.[13]

While shifting ocean currents could help explain the appearance of sargassum in new areas, warmer waters as well as increased nutrient loads might be creating ideal conditions for sargassum growth. Agricultural fertilizers, sewage, sediment from rivers, and even chemical dispersants from the BP oil spill can provide food for sargassum and other algae; the same nutrients cause the notorious dead zone at the mouth of the Mississippi River. As long as it finds nutrients, the sargassum will continue to grow. Researchers in Texas have documented masses of seaweed continuing to expand while floating in ocean currents and even suspended along the coast in front of local beaches.

Responses

Responses to the rise of sargassum have been varied, depending on the location, the extent of the problem, and the human and financial resources available. The Mexican government, responding to the potential loss of tourism dollars on the Yucatán coast, has confronted the problem with an almost military response, deploying the navy to find seaweed in the open ocean and investing over US $9 million in an army of beach cleaners.[14] With vast stretches of beach dedicated to tourism, Mexico cannot afford to lose tourists to seaweed. The language the Mexican government uses publicly even evokes thoughts of a war in which they are combatting an invading enemy that is "terrorizing" their tourism and beaches, and that must be "aggressively confronted."[15]

Other Caribbean nations have responded in various ways, again depending largely on the availability of resources. The region has seen a second invasion by a cottage industry of equipment vendors, entrepreneurs, and instant experts, all armed with solutions to rake seaweed off the beaches, convert it into some useful product, or protect beaches from sargassum with floating oil boom lines. Numerous resorts have installed floating barriers that minimize the arrival of sargassum to their beaches. All of the solutions proposed thus far are time consuming, labor intensive, expensive, and most likely temporary.

The Caribbean Hotel and Tourism Association (CHTA), working with the Caribbean Alliance for Sustainable Tourism (CAST), has published a guide for best practices to manage sargassum on hotel beaches.[16] The guide tends to focus on managing guest expectations while also trying to show the benefits of sargassum, such as its value in beach protection and its possible uses for fertilizer, compost, and landfill material. From a sustainability viewpoint, managing sargassum through large-scale mechanical removal can be one of the worst solutions, disrupting natural beach habitats and ecosystems while removing the potential benefits of seaweed. Some also see sargassum as a valuable educational resource for tourists. While the incoming red slick can be alarming to hotel managers, many of the species found hidden in the mats of seaweed are intricately evolved to camouflage in their habitat and can be quite exquisite.

The Future

Sargassum arrived quickly and without warning. It has proven difficult to predict and control. It has exacted devastating impacts on the local economies and ecosystems of the Caribbean and Mexico. And it appears to be caused by a complex, wide-ranging, and shifting set of factors that make preventing it challenging or even impossible. Whether the current landings will be a long-term problem related to global climate change or simply represent a short-term environmental challenge, the sargassum invasion is representative of other complex environmental challenges humans are currently facing, and will increasingly be forced to confront in the future. In the coming years, we will be embarking on a great experiment as we learn to adapt to rapid global changes, like sargassum seaweed, as part of the new normal.

Notes

1. The term *Sargassum* refers to a genus of brown macroalgae with some 300 individual species around the globe. The species most commonly found in the Atlantic and Caribbean are *S. natans* and *S. fluitans*. Source: The Seaweed Site. *Sargasso Sea*. Available at: http://www .seaweed.ie/sargassum/sargasso.php.
2. Michelle Higgins. (2011). Where's the beach? Under the seaweed. *New York Times*, October 11, 2011. Available at: http://www.nytimes .com/2011/10/16/travel/caribbean-beaches-dig-out-from-massive -seaweed-invasion.html.
3. Image Source: Martha Watkins Gilkes.
4. Anonymous. (2016). Nature Foundation warns: New Sargasso weed invasion underway. *Today: The Newspaper for Country St. Maarten*, February 23, 2016. Available at: http://www.todaysxm.com/nature -foundation-warns-new-sargasso-weed-invasion-underway/.
5. Anonymous. (2015). Sargassum seaweed, 'greatest single threat to the Caribbean tourism industry'. *MercoPress,* Wednesday, August 19, 2015. Available at: http://en.mercopress.com/2015/08/19/sargassum- seaweed-greatest-single-threat-to-the-caribbean-tourism-industry.
6. Joshua Partlow and Gabriella Martinez. (2015). Mexico deploys its navy to face its latest threat: Monster seaweed. *The Washington Post,* October 28, 2015. Available at: https://www.washingtonpost. com/world/the_americas/mexico-deploys-its-navy-to-face-its-latest- threat-monster-seaweed/2015/10/28/cea8ac28-710b-11e5-ba14 -318f8e87a2fc_story.html.

7. Ben Ellman. (2015). Caribbean choked by biggest seaweed bloom ever. *New York Magazine: Daily Intelligencer*, October 29, 2015. Available at: http://nymag.com/daily/intelligencer/2015/10/caribbean-choked-by-biggest-seaweed-bloom-ever.html.

8. Danny Lewis. (2015). Mexico's navy is battling seaweed along the Caribbean coast. *Smithsonian,* November 2, 2015. Available at: http://www.smithsonianmag.com/smart-news/mexicos-navy-battling-seaweed-along-caribbean-coast-180957112/.

9. Gay Nagle Myers. (2015). Caribbean, Mexico resorts plagued by sargassum outbreak. *Travel Weekly*, August 30, 2015. Available at: http://www.travelweekly.com/Mexico-Travel/Caribbean-and-Mexico-resorts-plagued-by-sargassum-outbreak.

10. Newswire. (2015). Caribbean looks to combat growing seaweed problem at local beaches. *Travel Agent Central,* July 4, 2015. Available at: http://www.travelagentcentral.com/caribbean/caribbean-looks-combat-growing-seaweed-problem-local-beaches-52296.

11. Sargasso Sea Commission. (2016). *About the Sargasso Sea.* Available at: http://www.sargassoseacommission.org/about-the-sargasso-sea.

12. Image Source: U.S. Fish and Wildlife Service.

13. Anne Broache. (2015). SEA research offers new insight on Caribbean seaweed invasion. *SEA Currents*, November 18, 2015. Sea Education Association. Available at: http://www.sea.edu/sea_currents/single/sea_researchers_publish_findings_on_caribbean_seaweed_invasion.

14. Joshua Partlow and Gabriella Martinez. (2015). Op cit.

15. Joshua Partlow and Gabriella Martinez. (2015). Op cit.

16. Caribbean Hotel & Tourism Association and Caribbean Alliance for Sustainable Tourism. (2015). *Sargassum: A Resource Guide for the Caribbean.* Available at: http://www.onecaribbean.org/wp-content/uploads/SargassumResourceGuideFinal.pdf.

CHAPTER 3

Fisheries, Tourism, and Climate Change

Overview—Marine Fisheries, Tourism, and Climate Impacts: Creating Opportunities for Change

Dawn M. Martin and Marida Hines

Introduction

Seafood is a critical food source for people around the world, particularly the residents of small island nations who depend upon healthy and abundant fisheries for their survival. More than three billion people rely on seafood as their primary source of protein, and nearly half a billion people derive their income from wild fisheries and fish farming, making seafood the largest traded food commodity in the world.[1] Annual per capita fish consumption increased from 9.9 kg in the 1960s to 19.2 kg today, nearly doubling in 50 years.[2] On top of this, global population is expected to reach 9.7 billion by 2050,[3] putting even more pressure on existing seafood supplies. To meet this demand, some have suggested that we must increase wild fisheries extraction as well as aquaculture production.

Unfortunately, the vast majority of wild fisheries are already at their limits. The United Nations Food and Agriculture Organization (FAO) estimates that 90 percent of ocean fisheries are either fully exploited (61 percent) or overfished (29 percent).[4] The FAO report concludes that, on average, stocks of commercially exploited fish declined some 50 percent in just 40 years, from 1970 to 2010, with some species like mackerel and tuna dropping even more precipitously. Climate change compounds these problems, as is already evident in tropical and subtropical regions such as the Caribbean. And well-documented declines of reef systems could have calamitous effects on regional fisheries.

The University of British Columbia's Nereus Program[5] has produced a recent report showing that the global supply of seafood is about to change substantially. Many people will not have access to reliable sources of seafood in the future due to climate change-related impacts on oceans. The report asserts that the world needs to aggressively combat rising greenhouse gas emissions and improve ocean governance to ensure the future of viable ocean fisheries. While some efforts to strengthen public policy have been made, more work is needed to respond to the complex challenges currently in play in the ocean and mitigate their impacts on vulnerable regions of the world, including the Caribbean.

As we describe in this essay, the tourism sector could have an important role to play in the future of global fisheries. Tourism has the ability to raise awareness, change public opinion, and shift consumer attitudes and behaviors. This in turn can pressure markets, influence policy, and improve the situation for people and economies that depend upon a healthy ocean. Rather than just contributing to the depletion of regional and global fish stocks, tourism can actually help to create demand for sustainable practices that lead to healthier and more sustainable fisheries.

Status of Fisheries and Impacts of Climate Change

Recent studies suggest that climate change is increasing stress on oceans already suffering from overfishing, pollution, and destruction of coastal and marine ecosystems.[6] Among the largest climate-related stressors are ocean acidification and sea temperature rise, both resulting from increased greenhouse gases in the atmosphere. As the ocean warms and becomes more acidic, ecosystem productivity is reduced, habitats are changed, and many species experience potentially devastating impacts on reproduction and survival.

As sea temperatures rise, ecosystem productivity tends to go down, particularly in tropical and subtropical regions such as the Caribbean. Some fish migrate to different areas, primarily to cooler waters, and since predators and prey do not always move in tandem, food chains can be disrupted.[7] Species unable to adapt or move may face extinction. Changing ocean temperatures could also have the effect of shifting ocean currents.[8] These forces may have been factors in several large-scale and catastrophic fishery crashes, including North Atlantic cod and herring, as well as the Peruvian anchoveta, California sardine, and Alaska king crab and pink shrimp. Changing sea currents might also factor into recent fluctuations in salmon numbers.[9]

Ocean acidification, where increasing amounts of carbon dioxide are making seawater more acidic, makes it difficult for mollusks, crabs, and corals to grow their shells.[10] Acidification mostly impacts species with calcareous (calcium carbonate) shells or exoskeletons, including lobsters, mussels, oysters, and other shellfish. Also affected are tiny organisms like pteropods that form the foundation of many marine food webs. Coral reefs, which serve as nurseries for juvenile fish, are among the ecosystems most vulnerable to ocean acidification. Calcification rates of coral reefs are projected to decline by 17 to 35 percent by 2100.[11] Freshwater spawning species like salmon are also impacted by ocean acidification, as heightened levels of CO_2 cause problems for fish reproduction and also impact digestion, hearing, and smelling, making it more difficult to find food or avoid predators.[12]

Meanwhile, the physical effects of climate change are also having major impacts on fisheries. An increase in the frequency and severity of ocean storms can damage critical marine habitats like coral reefs, mangroves, and seagrass beds.[13] Coral reefs and other fish nurseries are already being affected by rising sea levels, erosion, changing salinity levels, and changes in precipitation and sediment deposits. Extreme weather can affect the ability of fish to reproduce or migrate to spawning and feeding areas. Storms and other climate change patterns can also impact fishing infrastructure such as boat landing sites, processing facilities, transport routes, fish farms, and fishing communities.[14]

Aquaculture producers are also seeing impacts from climate-induced changes. Shellfish in particular are highly susceptible to disruptions such as changes in water temperature, lower oxygen levels, and increased

Image 3.0.1 A goliath grouper, one of the iconic fish species of the Caribbean, is highly susceptible to overfishing and is now protected in some areas[15]

acidity. Other climate-related impacts include the risk from more frequent and powerful coastal storms that can destroy offshore and onshore infrastructure such as holding pens and tank facilities. Meanwhile, there has not been adequate investment in aquaculture to grow the industry quickly enough to meet projected food needs.

Responses to Climate Change

Climate change's observed and predicted impacts on the world's oceans and fisheries require a response. Most obviously, CO_2 emissions must be controlled to reduce the rate and magnitude of ocean warming, sea level rise, acidification, and other changes in ocean properties. Ocean biodiversity and habitat must be protected to help marine ecosystems adapt to impacts from climate change and other human-induced stressors. Market systems need to support sustainable practices, but also be flexible enough to react to changes. More coordinated regulations will be needed among international fisheries. For example, as some species move to cooler waters, regulators may have to react quickly to keep resource allocation quotas aligned with new species distributions.

Industry Responses

The commercial fishing industry has reacted to reductions in fish populations mainly by investing in new technology that improves efficiency while refurbishing ships to enable them to travel farther and catch more diverse species. Such enhancements can improve fuel efficiency by allowing fishers to spend more time at sea, and improve product handling, storage, and preservation. Some smaller scale fishers are adapting by expanding their activities into aquaculture and tourism, and joining co-operatives and other risk-dispersing organizations.

As species available in a given region change, fishers are having to develop new harvesting strategies (for example, switching target species and gear), find ways to reduce bycatch of species new to their fishing grounds, and transition to new types of employment as commercial fishing becomes less economically viable. These changes are beginning to affect land-based support services from ports to processing plants. This may eventually force occupational changes upon whole regions and could increase social inequities and other problems, such as have been documented for North Atlantic cod fishing communities.[16]

Aquaculture, which applies commercial farming practices such as holding pens and artificial inputs to the raising of finfish and shellfish, holds great promise for delivering high-quality protein to a growing world population. However, aquaculture can also be impacted by climate change, as described above. Shellfish farmers are adapting in a variety of ways, including moving their shellfish to sites with cold water upwells, or lowering cages into cooler water. Future climate-related impacts, such as increased competition for water or flooding of coastal areas, may ultimately affect aquaculture operations and could lead to conflict between different sectors reliant on this resource.

Government and Nonprofit Responses

Most government, academic, and NGO adaptation programs in the seafood sector, meanwhile, have addressed resource depletion more directly than climate change. Those efforts are generally aimed at promoting biological resilience, rebuilding stocks, and reducing overcapacity in fishing fleets. For positive change to happen on the water, however, one of the first steps will be to encourage the seafood sector to focus explicitly on climate change in addition to combating the depletion of fisheries.

Government policy and regulatory decision-makers have tended to focus on protecting fish resources by implementing quotas and using ecosystem-based fisheries management. Marine reserves, fishery improvement projects (FIPs), and strategies to prevent habitat loss such as destruction of mangroves (which serve as fish nurseries) are increasing globally. Governments and academic institutions are supporting research that can improve fisheries management in the face of climate change. This includes examining the effect of sea temperature rise on species and their prey, predators, and competitors. The public sector can also play a role by improving climate change research, responding to disasters, and improving communication and information sharing on climate change and fisheries.

Tourism Sector Response

There are encouraging signs from both large corporations and small local businesses that the tourism industry is stepping into a new role as ambassadors for sustainability. Several trends show resourcefulness in responding to the challenges of climate change and fisheries. A growing *locavore* (based on foods from the surrounding area) seafood movement tied to the hospitality industry can help reduce the carbon footprint of fishing and lead to more sustainable practices. Many chefs have begun to promote sustainable seafood and have taken unsustainable items such as shark fin soup off their menus.

Resort restaurants are well positioned to educate consumers about the benefits of sustainable seafood, including consumption of more abundant or invasive species, as well as nonfish seafood such as seaweed, while also bringing to light the impacts of climate change on vacation and resort destinations. Some hotels and resorts are already implementing sustainable seafood policies and training their staff to source from local fishers, bringing economic drivers into their communities and providing local stories about the fish that are served. For example, Marriott International's Future Fish program is designed to help the company's hotels source, cook, and serve sustainable seafood.[17] Morgan's Rock Hacienda and Ecolodge in Nicaragua features sustainable seafood including shrimp from a local organic shrimp farm and catch from local fishermen who use traditional fishing methods in nearby waters.

Promoting sustainable tourism to fishing villages, and familiarizing visitors with the fishing lifestyle, could help provide economic alternatives for communities while building awareness of this sector. The locavore movement could be expanded using such mechanisms as community supported fisheries (CSFs) to support and tell the story of local and sustainably caught or farmed seafood. Where possible, commercial and recreational fishers should work together to support sustainable fisheries management. Local restaurants, resorts, and retail stores could develop brands that focus on fish from responsibly managed local sources, such as the Gulf of Maine Research Institute's Out of the Blue and Trawl to Table programs. A number of other seafood certification programs around the world could be looked at as examples for the Caribbean.

Tourism as a Tool for Change

Historically, the conservation community has not fully utilized the social sciences to help understand and modify human behavior and beliefs regarding climate change.[18] Only about 2 percent of all climate change research dollars are spent on changing human behavior, even though it is widely recognized as the most important factor in dealing with this issue.[19] Research shows that for information about climate change to be absorbed by the public, it must be communicated with appropriate language and narrative storytelling made vivid through imagery and experiential scenarios, balanced with scientific information delivered by trusted messengers.[20] While this approach has not been fully applied to ocean education, it has been successfully applied to other aspects of climate change.

It is difficult to explain how important the ocean is to our well-being, or how fragile it actually is. The public generally has an outdated perception of the ocean, viewing it as immense, bountiful, inexhaustible, infinitely resilient, and impervious to human influence. The media and conservation organizations also tend to present doom and gloom scenarios laden with jargon that the general public does not understand. As a result, the information and messages conveyed either do not resonate with the public, or scare people into inaction.

Most people also experience marine conservation issues from a distance, having little personal experience with oceans or fisheries to draw upon, and seeing things like climate change as someone else's problem, or a problem for the future. As a result, threats to the ocean, including the complex, largely invisible, and seemingly overwhelming effects of climate change, are difficult to convey in a way that resonates with the public and that they can easily understand. Despite the dominance of the ocean on our planet, only a small percentage of people have actually seen the underwater environment. As social science has shown, however, it is often emotional responses rather than scientific theories or abstract models that lead to behavioral changes.

The tourism industry can serve a valuable role by connecting people to their surroundings, evoking an emotional response that leads to conservation action. By providing access to ocean environments and fisheries, marine tourism provides an opportunity to advance sustainability through behavioral change. The tourism industry can also help create more sustainable fisheries by joining a comprehensive strategic communications effort to transform attitudes and behaviors related to climate change, overfishing, and depletion of marine species. More research is needed, however, to determine how tourism and fisheries can work together to influence the opinions, attitudes, and behaviors of consumers.

Conclusion

Tourism in the Caribbean is well placed to create meaningful change if it joins with the fishing industry and local communities to use strategic communication methods to change hearts and minds. Tourists can be influenced by strategic messaging focused on protecting the places they choose to visit and enjoy while on vacation. A comprehensive plan rooted in these strategies would be extremely beneficial in identifying and implementing action steps that can be taken across sectors, and throughout the islands in the Caribbean, to address these issues.

A key first step would be to synthesize and address human psychological and behavioral dimensions with respect to conservation of the ocean and the life it supports by: (a) engaging experts in fields such as psychology, anthropology, communications, marketing and branding, economics, history, and environmental and marine science and policy; (b) illuminating the motivators of human behavior to improve and implement targeted marine conservation, management and policy efforts; and (c) developing practical approaches for modifying behavior with respect to marine environments and critical issues such as ocean acidification. This strategy could help bridge the gap that now exists between ocean issues and the communities impacted by climate change, connecting them in an intelligent and strategic way, and filtering the noise that permeates our society. It would also help ensure that targeted audiences receive clear, meaningful, and understandable messages that will resonate and lead to meaningful change.

Compared to other animal protein sources, seafood is a highly efficient food source with a relatively low carbon footprint.[21] For this reason, the fishing industry, as well as related tourism sectors that rely on fisheries, could be on the front lines of an education and outreach effort regarding climate change. In so doing, they could position seafood as the best option for animal protein both in terms of human health and in its comparatively small contribution to climate change. And they could help the many coastal communities that rely on both fishing and tourism, in the Caribbean and beyond, to weather the coming storm of climate change.

Notes

1. Statistics in this section are drawn largely from: Worldwide Fund for Nature. (2015). *Living Blue Planet Report: Species, Habitats and Human Well-being.* London, UK: WWF International and Institute of Zoology, Zoological Society of London. Available at: http://assets.wwf.org.uk/downloads/living_blue_planet_report_2015.pdf.
2. FAO. (2014). *The State of World Fisheries and Aquaculture.* Rome, Italy: Food and Agriculture Organization of the United Nations. Available at: http://www.fao.org/3/a-i3720e.pdf.

3. United Nations. (2015). *World Population Prospects: The 2015 Revision, Key Findings and Advance Tables*. Working Paper No. ESA/P/WP.241. UN Department of Economic and Social Affairs, Population Division. Available at: https://esa.un.org/unpd/wpp/Publications/Files /Key_Findings_WPP_2015.pdf.

4. FAO. (2014). Op cit.

5. University of British Columbia. (2016). *Nereus Program.* Available at: http://www.nereusprogram.org/.

6. Donald Scavia, John Field, Donald Boesch, Robert Buddemeier, Virginia Burkett, Daniel Cayan, Michael Fogarty, Mark Harwell, Robert Howarth, Curt Mason, Denise Reed, Thomas Royer, Asbury Sallenger, and James Titus. (2002). Climate Change Impacts on U.S. Coastal and Marine Ecosystems. *Estuaries*, 25(2), 149–164. Available at: http://tenaya.ucsd.edu/~cayan/Pubs/66_Scavia_Estuaries _2002.pdf.

7. Marine Stewardship Council. (2016). *Climate Change and Fish.* Available at: https://www.msc.org/healthy-oceans/the-oceans-today /climate-change.

8. Stefan Rahmstorf. (2006). Thermohaline Ocean Circulation. In S.A. Elias, ed. *Encyclopedia of Quaternary Sciences.* Amsterdam: Elsevier. Available at: http://pik-potsdam.de/~stefan/Publications /Book_chapters/rahmstorf_eqs_2006.pdf.

9. Terry Johnson. (2012). *Fisheries Adaptations to Climate Change.* SeaGrant Alaska. Available at: http://seagrant.noaa.gov/Portals/0 /Documents/what_we_do/climate/AK%20SG%20Fisheries %20Adaptations%20to%20Climate%20Change.pdf.

10. Michael Casey. (2015). Climate change could drain global seafood supplies. *CBS News online.* Available at: http://www.cbsnews.com/ news/global-seafood-supplies-may-be-hit-by-climate-change/.

11. Donald Scavia, et al. (2002). Op cit.

12. Mark Fischetti. (2012). Ocean Acidification Can Mess with a Fish's Mind. *Scientific American*, September 27, 2012. Available at: http:// www.scientificamerican.com/article/ocean-acidification-can-m/.

13. WWF. (2014). Op cit.

14. U. Rashid Sumaila, William Cheung, Vicky Lam, Daniel Pauly, and Samuel Herrick. (2011). Climate Change Impacts on the

Biophysics and Economics of World Fisheries. *Nature Climate Change*, November 11, 2011. Available at: http://vintage.joss.ucar .edu/cwg/july12/Sumaila_2011.pdf.

15. Image Source: Bill Goodwin, NOAA.

16. Dean Bavington. (2010). *Managed Annihilation: An Unnatural History of the Newfoundland Cod Collapse.* Vancouver: UBC Press.

17. Amy Sung. (2011). Marriott International's 'Future Fish' steers menu and chef choices. *FSR Magazine*. Available at: https://www .fsrmagazine.com/content/marriott-international-s-future-fish -steers-menu-and-chef-choices.

18. Robert Gifford. (2008). Psychology's Essential Role in Alleviating the Impacts of Climate Change. *Canadian Psychology*, 49(4), 273–80.

19. Center for Research on Environmental Decisions. (2009). *The Psychology of Climate Change Communication: A Guide for Scientists, Journalists, Educators, Political Aides, and the Interested Public.* New York: Center for Research on Environmental Decisions, Columbia University.

20. Center for Research on Environmental Decisions. (2009). Op cit.

21. Eartheasy. (2011). Eco-impact of wild seafood less than that of poultry, beef. *Eartheasy: Solutions for Sustainable Living*. Available at: http://learn.eartheasy.com/2011/02/eco-impact-of-wild-seafood -less-than-that-of-poultry-beef/.

Case Study 3.1

Masyarakat dan Perikanen Indonesia (MDPI) Foundation: Supporting Coastal Fishing Community Resilience Through Tourism

by Marida Hines and Dawn M. Martin

Many Caribbean and other small island developing nations face challenges to building financially sound, sustainable, small-scale artisanal fisheries. This case study highlights an easily adopted model for a fishing/tourism alliance that strengthens the viability of fishing communities facing the effects of climate change. For tourists, this means being treated to delicious, high-quality seafood while helping build economic and environmental resilience in the communities where they choose to vacation. For fishers who rely on ocean resources facing increased stress from climate change, it provides a framework for introducing sustainable seafood to the public in a nonthreatening setting where they are receptive to the message.

Masyarakat dan Perikanen Indonesia (MDPI), roughly translated as "Communities and Fisheries of Indonesia," supports the fishing industry with sustainability projects and on-the-ground implementation. They also work with seafood buyers and distributors to identify what aspects of sustainability and traceability they are interested in, so they can tailor their programs to meet the needs of the market and get the most benefit for the fishing communities with which they work.

The Origins of MDPI

In 2010, Anova Food, an international supplier of fresh and frozen seafood, launched a pilot program in a fishing village in Indonesia that would have far-reaching effects. The "Fishing & Living" program's goal was to introduce local community-based fishers to a more sustainable and responsible kind of fishing, improving practices in longline fisheries and opening new markets for their sustainable catch.[1] Fishing & Living's novel approach was to not just address the environmental aspects of fisheries but also to promote local community development and the well-being of fishers. This comprehensive approach to sustainability won Anova's Fishing & Living program a SeaWeb Seafood Champion Award for Innovation in 2015.[2]

Anova's work started with teaching sustainable fishing concepts to local university students and placing them in permanently staffed Fisher Centers in small villages. These centers implemented social programs, conducted beach cleanups, prepared safety-at-sea guidebooks, raised conservation awareness, developed alternative livelihood programs, and created a pilot project for implementing fair trade standards for capture fisheries. One result was Indonesian Handline Yellowfin Tuna (*Thunnus albacares*), certified through Fair Trade USA.[3] Efforts beyond the water's edge included donations to local schools and orphanages such as books, sporting equipment, water filtration systems, and English classes.

The World's First Fair Trade Certified Wild-Caught Fishery

The pilot program was such a success that in 2013 it was spun off into an independent nonprofit organization called Masyarakat Dan Perikanan

Image 3.1.1 The Fair Trade Fisher association, Tuna Lestari (Everlasting Tuna), completing its first official meeting, voting and inauguration of association positions, Ambon Island, the Moluccas[4]

Indonesia (MDPI), or "Communities and Fisheries of Indonesia."[5] MDPI's vision for a better future, like its parent organization, includes improving both the health of fisheries and the coastal communities that rely on them. The organization provides scientific, social, and community development activities for fishing communities, including sessions on sea-food safety and quality, adopt-a-school events, and the implementation of clean-water systems in schools and orphanages.

MDPI formed data management committees and fisheries data collection programs around Indonesia to gather information on interactions with endangered, protected, and threatened species. MDPI also works with fisheries to improve traceability, development of localized management systems, and improvements to fishing methods through fisheries improvement projects (FIPs). In 2014, a collaboration between MDPI and three fishers associations in the Moluccan Islands led to Moluccan Yellowfin Tuna becoming the first Fair Trade Certified™ wild-caught fish in the world.[6]

These successes are increasing the resilience of both fisheries and the fishers who depend on them as they confront the added stresses caused by climate change. They are all the more meaningful because they are taking

Image 3.1.2 Wildan and Imran, MDPI enumerators, collecting data from a handline tuna fisher in Maumere, East Nusa Tenggara[7]

Image 3.1.3 Stephani of MDPI training a group of new data collection enumerators in Buru Island, the Moluccas[8]

place in a small island developing state, as well as an area of the world known for pirate fishing and human rights abuses in the international fishing fleet.

A Fisheries Catch-22

To maintain the progress they had made, MDPI managers had to convince more local fisheries to work toward certification. To do so, they needed to demonstrate that increasing sustainability also increased access to markets. Until the number of fisheries achieving certification increased, however, the volume of fish was too small to interest international buyers. It was in this context that, in February 2015, a representative of MDPI received a scholarship to participate in the SeaWeb Seafood Summit in New Orleans.

The Summit is an annual international conference that brings together global representatives from the seafood industry with leaders from the conservation community, academia, government, and the media. Together they work to define success and advance solutions in sustainable seafood through dialogue and partnerships that lead to a seafood marketplace that is environmentally, socially, and economically sustainable.

The scholarship recipient was Momo Kochen, Director of Research and Programs at MDPI. Her experience implementing grassroots campaigns in a developing nation brought a valuable perspective to the summit, where she spoke on a panel entitled "Certification, Traceability, and Consumer Awareness in the Global South." She also represented MDPI at the annual Seafood Champion Awards, where they were finalists in the Vision category.

During each summit, scholars such as Momo are paired with mentors who help them overcome obstacles in their efforts to build sustainable fisheries in their regions of the world. One of Momo's goals for her scholarship was to meet and learn from others implementing FIPs. She was teamed with the president of the nonprofit organization Centro Desarrollo Y Pesca Sustentable (Center for Development and Sustainable Fisheries),[9] Ernesto Godelman, who was able to give her the benefit of his experience implementing FIPs in Argentina, Mexico, Brazil, Chile, Panama, and Guatemala.

The issue Momo was most passionate about was finding markets for fish from traceability pilot programs that MDPI had put in place in Indonesia. Her ongoing efforts to find buyers for her sustainable seafood—including a trip to the United States where she spoke in person to retailers across the country—had yielded no solutions. "Every buyer was willing, but each wanted someone else to take the first step," she lamented. Without an established market for MDPI's sustainably caught fish, it would be an uphill battle to expand sustainable practices to more fisheries in Indonesia. "The fishermen need to see a benefit" for their commitment to sustainability, she insisted.

From Boat to Bali: A Win–Win Situation

On the second day of the summit, Momo was introduced to Ned Bell, executive chef at Four Seasons Restaurant in Vancouver, Canada. Ned is a passionate sustainable seafood advocate. His restaurant leads by example: their seafood menu is deemed 100 percent sustainable through

Image 3.1.4 Harjo, MDPI enumerator, interviewing a fisherman on the details of his trip, Buru Island, the Moluccas[10]

its consistency with the recommendations of Vancouver Aquarium's Ocean Wise[11] program, and the staff is fully educated about sustainable seafood. Ned is also the founder of Chefs for Oceans,[12] a campaign to engage and inspire chefs and communities to source seafood sustainably. One of Chefs for Oceans' strategies is to encourage restaurants to source directly from sustainable small-scale producers.

Ned and Momo spoke at length during the summit, and Momo returned to Indonesia with a plan. She has now established alliances with a growing number of high-end restaurants in Bali, Indonesia, to purchase MDPI's certified seafood and promote it to their clientele of affluent Indonesians and international tourists. As this plan expands, it will serve as a bridge to allow small certified fisheries to grow, and newly certified fisheries to realize a premium on their sustainability efforts.

Summary

Masyarakat Dan Perikanan Indonesia brings the fishing and tourism sectors together to help communities overcome the threats of climate change. Meanwhile, the Caribbean, with its many high-end resorts, is well placed to benefit from a communications campaign similar to MDPI's and those SeaWeb has implemented elsewhere. This includes using prominent chefs as spokespersons to protect at-risk species and achieve both market-based and policy solutions in support of sustainability. SeaWeb's work with chefs, caterers, and restaurateurs has demonstrated the valuable role culinary leaders can play in advancing seafood sustainability, not only by sourcing seafood sustainably and through the choice of species they serve, but also by using their status to educate consumers.

Notes

1. Fishing & Living. (2016). *Improving Life in the Fishing Community*. Available at: http://fishing-living.org/#sthash.03Y4r1d6.dpbs.
2. SeaWeb. (2015). Seafood Champion Award. *Anova Food's Fishing and Living*. Available at: http://www.seafoodchampions.org/2015-seafood-champions/anova-foods-fishing-living/#more-365.
3. Fair Trade USA. (2016). *Producer Profiles*: *Coral Triangle Processors-Malukus*. Available at: http://fairtradeusa.org/producer-profiles/coral-triangle-processors-malukus.
4. Image Source: MDPI.
5. Masyarakat Dan Perikanan Indonesia. (2016). *Who we are*. Available at: http://mdpi.or.id/index.php/about-us.
6. Fair Trade USA. (2016). Op cit.
7. Image Source: MDPI.
8. Image Source: MDPI.
9. Centro Desarrollo y Pesca Sustentable (CeDePesca). (2016). *Home page*. Available at: http://cedepesca.net/.
10. Image Source: MDPI.
11. Vancouver Aquarium. (2016). *Ocean Wise*. Available at: http://www.oceanwise.ca.
12. Chefs for Oceans. (2016). *Mission*. Available at: http://chefsforoceans.com.

Case Study 3.2

Working with Industry to Protect Marine Fisheries: The Gulf of Maine Research Institute's Sustainable Seafood Initiative

by Jen Levin

The Gulf of Maine Research Institute (GMRI) is a neutral nonprofit supporting economic and ecological sustainability in the Gulf of Maine and beyond. Located in Portland, Maine, USA, GMRI conducts world-class marine science, fosters relationships with working fishing communities, and creates immersive science education programs. We are committed to core principles of objectivity and collaboration.

GMRI's work is organized in four focus areas: stewarding ecosystems, cultivating science literacy, supporting sustainable seafood, and strengthening coastal communities. Our primary services include scientific research; technical assistance for the region's fishing industry, resource managers, and seafood businesses; and structured education programs for middle school students and their teachers.

The Gulf of Maine is warming faster than 99 percent of the world's oceans, and this has created special challenges to marine fisheries and coastal communities in this region. GMRI scientists are working hard to understand how the physical changes over the last few decades affect the ecosystem. We have seen shifts in the timing and composition of key zooplankton species, changes in when and where commercial species (including lobster) are caught, dramatic declines of cold water species such as cod and shrimp, and an influx of southerly species like black sea bass and green crabs, both of which prey on commercially harvested species like lobsters and clams. To respond to these changes, we integrate research from many different disciplines to develop solutions that allow fisheries managers and fishing communities to become more resilient in the face of changing ocean conditions.

Gulf of Maine
Research Institute
Science. Education. Community.

© *Gulf of Maine Research Institute*

GMRI's Sustainable Seafood Programs

The Gulf of Maine Research Institute has shown exceptional commitment to marine research, fisheries improvement, and the convening of seafood stakeholders to improve the sustainability of seafood and ocean health in the region. GMRI's Sustainable Seafood Initiative and Marine Resource Education Program (MREP) in particular have established the organization as a leader in the field by successfully bringing together harvesters, policy makers, fisheries managers, scientists, conservation organizations, processors, wholesalers, distributors, academic and corporate institutions, restaurateurs, and major retailers to find solutions to the complex challenges facing ocean health and the seafood industry today.

The Sustainable Seafood Initiative works with a diverse group of stakeholders to meet the unique challenges and opportunities of the Gulf of Maine fisheries and coastal communities. By working with all parts of the supply chain, the initiative creates a system that rewards fisheries, farms, and seafood companies that are committed to reducing their ecological impacts. Current projects include five major areas related to sustainable fisheries: (a) our work with supermarkets through Delhaize America, (b) the Gulf of Maine Responsibly Harvested brand program, (c) the Culinary Partners Program, (d) Out of the Blue, and (e) Trawl to Table.

Delhaize America Initiatives

Since 2009, GMRI has worked with Delhaize America supermarkets, which include 1,700 stores under Hannaford and Food Lion banners, to develop and implement a sustainable seafood sourcing policy. The policy covers all seafood products in the store, including fresh, frozen, and canned items. The policy requires that sourced fisheries are regulated by a credible management body, that enough science exists to determine sustainable harvest levels, that harvests are monitored, and that rules are enforced. The policy also requires that all seafood is traceable to the source and all fisheries are assessed individually, making this one of the most comprehensive seafood sourcing initiatives in North America. GMRI's role has been to inform the policy and work with Delhaize's suppliers to ensure their products meet the criteria outlined. This has required the continuous involvement of scientists, management bodies, Delhaize representatives, and certifying agencies.

Gulf of Maine Responsibly Harvested® Brand

The Gulf of Maine Responsibly Harvested® (GoMRH) branding program motivates improvements in the sustainability of our seafood industry by capitalizing on consumer preferences for responsibly harvested products from a known place. Ten species, five of which are significantly underutilized, currently receive the brand seal at large retail locations, helping customers to support local and regional fisheries at the seafood counter. In 2015, GMRI's Seafood Program participated in over 20 events to increase consumer awareness of and value for Gulf of Maine seafood, and to implement marketing plans to increase harvesting of underutilized species. GoMRH branded products can now be found at major retailers such as Hannaford and Shaw's supermarkets, as well as institutions including colleges, company cafeterias, and food service companies.

Research has shown that consumers prefer to know where their food is harvested and are concerned with its sustainability. All products that carry the GoMRH brand are verified by GMRI as being responsibly harvested and having third party verification that they are traceable to the Gulf of Maine. A traceability pilot is being explored to enable regional fishermen to distinguish themselves to increase the value of their landings. As part of this pilot, GMRI has been working with fishermen, dealers, retailers, and traceability platform providers to document barriers and benefits of boat-to-plate traceability of their products. A seafood traceability app is a component of this work.

Culinary Partners Program

The Culinary Partners Program works directly with restaurants and chefs to inform seafood decision-making and connect them with sustainable seafood from the Gulf of Maine. GMRI Culinary Partners commit to having at least 20 percent of their seafood sourced from the region, having at least one GoMRH verified species on the menu at all times, improving on their environmental footprint, attending staff education seminars, and sharing sustainable seafood information with their customers. Americans eat the majority of their seafood at restaurants, so by working with chefs, the middle of the supply chain, and harvesters directly, GMRI has generated an avenue for direct impact on what seafood consumers are aware of and exposed to, thereby influencing market demand in an observable manner.

Out of the Blue

GMRI features several efforts to raise awareness of and value for under-utilized, lesser-known species in the Gulf of Maine, with the goal of diversifying what is marketable and profitable for fishermen while reducing impacts on more vulnerable or over-harvested species. The Institute has coordinated with over 40 regional chefs to build markets for underutilized Gulf of Maine seafood species during 10-day and month-long promotions known as Out of the Blue. This program uses direct marketing and print materials, social media campaigns, and news media coverage in local papers, televised segments, and radio announcements to encourage diners to seek out these species at area restaurants. Out of the Blue works alongside the Culinary Partners program to help restaurants support the region's fishing industry by always having local seafood items on the menu and educating staff and customers about these choices.

Trawl to Table

Trawl to Table connects chefs with fishermen and fisheries scientists for daylong events to work through difficulties in the supply chain. Participants learn about fishing gear technology, tour fish processing facilities, and attend presentations on quality handling techniques and strategies for sustainability. In 2014, GMRI hosted 3 Trawl to Table events throughout New England, with 2 events in 2015. In total, 174 fishermen, chefs, suppliers, institutions, and retailers have attended Trawl to Table events in Massachusetts, New Hampshire, and Maine to learn about seafood sustainability, quality handling, processing, and distribution, and how to increase the overall value and resilience of the Gulf of Maine seafood industry.

Image 3.2.2 GMRI Fishing Gear Technologist Steve Eayrs leading a discussion at a Trawl to Table event[1]

Other Programs

GMRI engages in other projects that support sustainable fisheries management in the Gulf of Maine by bringing together stakeholders to discuss management policies, fishing techniques and equipment, and scientific knowledge. Some of these are described briefly below.

Marine Resource Education Program

The Marine Resource Education Program (MREP) arose from ongoing conversations among fishing community leaders active in the New England fishery management process. MREP was conceived, managed, and presented by fishermen, for fishermen, with GMRI as the organizing body. MREP was formed to address the question, What do fishermen need to know to be effective participants in collaborative science and management? Offered annually, with over 500 graduates to date, MREP has received recognition for raising the knowledge base within the Northeast U.S. fishing community. The program recognizes the valuable information that fishermen have and promotes cooperative efforts between fishermen, managers, and scientists to address complex fishery issues. Since its inception in 2001, MREP has expanded to the Southeast, Gulf of Mexico, and Caribbean fisheries, with programs tailored to the unique fisheries and management processes of those regions. MREP recognizes the valuable information fishermen contribute and provides a platform for industry and science collaborations.

Fishery Improvement Projects

GMRI has spearheaded two fishery improvement projects (FIPs) in the Gulf of Maine region, connecting harvesters with policy makers, scientists, and major industry players to develop fisheries management, stock assessment, and marketing plans. The first FIP was for the Jonah crab, a species that was previously unregulated and the sustainability of which was unknown. GMRI is also facilitating the potential development of an FIP for winter skate, a product that is primarily landed in the region and shipped to Europe for consumption. By convening various parties, GMRI has helped protect the environmental and economic sustainability of these species.

FTAP and GEARNET

The Fisheries Technical Assistance Program (FTAP) was developed to combine GMRI's extensive work with New England groundfish sectors and our broadening outreach efforts into other fisheries and fisheries management related issues. Providing a range of technical, convening, and outreach services to New England's commercial fishing industry, FTAP supports 17 groundfish sectors through workshop and training offerings.

The Gear Conservation Engineering and Demonstration Network (GEARNET) works directly with fishermen and engineers, developing, trialing, and implementing new fishing gear technologies that improve the sustainability of seafood resources as well as the fishing industry. Improvements have included reduced fuel use in trawl tows, significantly reduced bycatch in nets, and decreased sea-bottom and ecosystem impacts.

Conclusion

Climate change is just one of many factors affecting the sustainability of fisheries in the Gulf of Maine, as well as in other places like the Caribbean.

Through scientific research, outreach, policy, and education efforts, the Gulf of Maine Research Institute is helping communities and the fishing industry respond to these changes and protect the species and ecosystems on which they depend. With its innovative and collaborative approach, GMRI has emerged as a leader in organizing multiple stakeholders to improve the sustainability of seafood and ocean health. Our website, www.gmri.org, provides more details on these efforts.

Note

1. Image Source: Gulf of Maine Research Institute.

CHAPTER 4

Marine Protected Areas as Climate Change Buffers and Tourism Magnets

Overview—Ocean-based Tourism and Marine Protected Areas: Opportunities for Engagement and Enhanced Resilience

Chiara Zuccarino-Crowe

Introduction

Marine protected areas (MPAs) conserve some of the most beautiful and biologically diverse places on our planet. Although the stressors associated with tourism can pose serious threats to marine and coastal environments, engagement with the tourism industry also provides a platform for MPA managers to raise the visibility of their sites and share conservation priorities. This outreach is crucial given the added stress that climate change imposes on the marine realm and ocean-dependent communities. Each visitor to an MPA represents an opportunity to educate the public about resource protection and management practices that build capacity for sustainable ocean tourism and enhance resilience against the impacts of climate change. The experiences visitors enjoy within special ocean places are an important part of fostering a sense of stewardship and generating much-needed support for climate-smart conservation.

Defining Marine Protected Areas

Marine Protected Areas (MPAs) involve the place-based conservation of ocean resources and environments. To quote a more technical perspective, an MPA can be broadly defined as "any area of intertidal or subtidal terrain, together with its overlying water and associated flora, fauna, historical and cultural features, which has been reserved by law or other effective means to protect part or all of the enclosed environment."[1] MPAs are called by a diverse range of names, such as national marine sanctuaries, coastal or marine parks, marine managed areas, reserves, wilderness areas, refuges, and more. When a series of MPAs is designed and managed to meet objectives in a coordinated way to accomplish more than individual sites can achieve, it is referred to as an MPA network.[2]

There is substantial diversity in the scope and scale of MPAs, as levels of protection, size, conservation foci, management approaches, and governing bodies vary widely. In just the U.S. and its territories, for example, more than 100 legal authorities have been involved in establishing over 1,700 MPAs.[3] The primary reasons for MPA designation include conservation of natural heritage or ecological value, protection of cultural

Image 4.0.1 Majestic humpback whales[4]

heritage, and sustainable production or restoration of marine resources such as fisheries.

This range of conservation priorities means that MPAs are located across a variety of marine habitats and can be designed to encompass unique features or a specific ecosystem function. This leads to a diversity of sizes, with MPAs ranging from as small as 0.4 sq. mi. (1 km²) to more than 463,000 sq. mi. (1.2 million km²).[5] There are more than 17,000 MPAs worldwide, covering a total area of about 4.75 million sq. mi. (12.3 million km²).[6] This means that approximately 3.4 percent of the world's ocean is recorded as being under some level of protection. This is far less than international conservation targets for marine protection, however, which range from 10 percent[7] to 30 percent[8] of the ocean, depending on the organization and context for discussion.

Most MPAs allow multiple uses, with some permitting closely managed extractive activities and others prohibiting all forms of consumptive uses. No-take areas, often referred to as marine reserves, are a type of MPA in which any harvest of marine life is prohibited. A few areas restrict human access to protect sensitive resources such as bird nesting areas or marine mammal haul-outs. These higher levels of protection are quite rare, however, with only 0.59 percent of the world's oceans, or about 17 percent of all protected areas, contained in no-take reserves.[9]

When protective measures potentially impact people's livelihoods, especially in more restrictive situations, MPAs can become the subject of debate because of the diverse interests and values at stake.[10] This controversy can be fueled by questions regarding economic impacts and MPA effectiveness, especially because external conditions such as pollution, invasive species, and climate change can also affect how well an MPA succeeds in its intended functions. The availability of resources and extent of enforcement capabilities can further impact whether an MPA's goals are achieved. Effective management is paramount to realizing the full benefits and minimizing the costs for both local communities and the marine environment.[11]

Why are MPAs Important?

MPAs provide a variety of benefits to marine systems and human communities: they can conserve biodiversity, protect natural or cultural heritage, enhance fisheries production, provide reference areas for research,

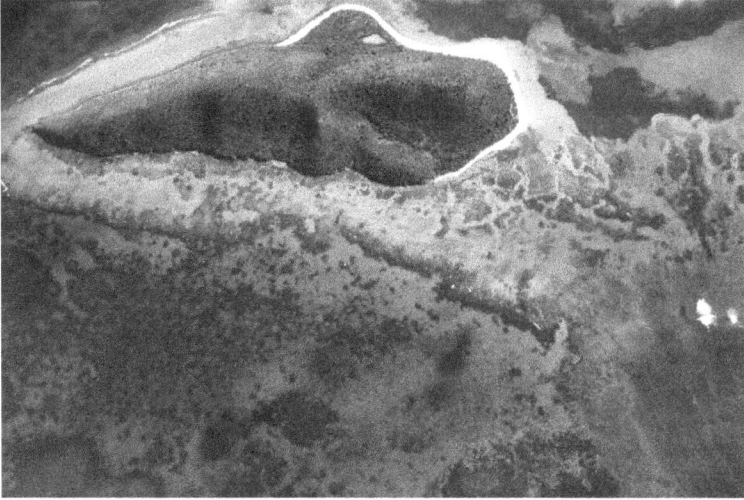

Image 4.0.2 Buck Island Reef National Monument, located in the U.S. Virgin Islands, is one of many MPAs found in the Caribbean region[12]

and promote ocean literacy, among other things. The use of marine protected areas as conservation tools is an application of the precautionary principle, since they provide insurance against uncertainty in other marine resource management approaches. MPAs also can provide significant ecosystem services, such as when protected coral reefs dissipate wave action and reduce shoreline erosion, protecting coastal properties. In this way, individual MPAs and especially well-designed MPA networks contribute to increased system resilience in the face of other stressors, whether ecological or socioeconomic. This resilience is especially important as it relates to the main subjects of this publication: climate change and tourism.

Climate Change and MPAs

Impacts associated with climate change can threaten environments and resources within MPAs. Increased water temperatures, rising sea levels, ocean acidification, changes in oceanic circulation and weather patterns, and increased storm activity all exert stress on these special places. Of primary concern is how this affects the ability of protected areas to function as designed. For example, if an MPA is meant to provide a sanctuary for threatened species, and warming water temperatures cause those species to permanently relocate to other areas with preferred temperature ranges, the original MPA ceases to serve its intended purpose. The same logic applies to objectives like habitat conservation.

At the same time, marine protected areas can help mitigate climate change in a direct manner through increased carbon sequestration via protection and restoration of key habitats that serve as carbon sinks, like seagrass beds and mangroves.[13] Indirectly, MPAs can help reduce future climate change impacts by inspiring visitors to act as better stewards and modify their own actions. MPAs frequently have outreach and education programs that engage external audiences, including tourists. These education programs can help spur behavioral change to reduce local impacts to marine resources.

While education related to climate and ocean literacy can contribute to resilience, the ability to restrict activities that stress marine environments, and to protect key species and habitats, are the cornerstones of how MPAs build ecological resilience to climate change. The legal and regulatory frameworks of MPAs are critical to limiting local non-climate associated stressors. The ability of MPA managers to apply planning and management actions to address impacts related to climate change will play a key role in the future of MPAs. This begins with the design of MPAs and MPA networks that encompass a diversity of species and habitats likely to withstand catastrophic losses associated with extreme events.[14] It also includes science programs that support monitoring and research related to understanding climate change impacts and trends.

MPA managers have a responsibility to apply the concept of *climate-smart conservation*. This approach requires many of the tenets already considered best management practices for MPAs. In addition, effective managers must account for uncertainty, anticipate surprises, understand the difference between climate variability and climate change in management planning, make contributions to the larger global effort to reduce the rate and extent of climate change, and take steps to reduce non-climate stresses.

MPAs and Sustainable Tourism

The unique natural and cultural resources often contained within MPAs make them prime destinations for visitors who support local recreation and tourism industries. Of the 35 distinct ocean-use categories described by NOAA's National MPA Center, for example, 20 have a recreational purpose and support tourism industries.[15] Recreational fishing, diving, surfing, swimming, and boating are all activities that tourists are more likely to enjoy in an ecologically healthy and responsibly managed location. An abundance of fish to catch makes for a more productive sport fishing outing. Beautiful coral reefs with diverse marine life to observe provide stimulating snorkeling opportunities. Scuba divers will appreciate, and flock to, well-preserved shipwrecks they can explore, while surfers and beachgoers prefer waters free of pollution and harmful algal blooms. Visitors seeking coastal destinations expect picturesque open horizons to gaze at from land or sea. These positive experiences are what keep tourists coming. In the Caribbean, half of all recreational diving happens in MPAs, highlighting the integral connection between tourism and the desirable marine resources found in protected areas.[16]

Tourism generated through MPAs can make protected areas more attractive to local communities, increasing their acceptance in places like the Caribbean.[17, 18] In some cases, the potential income lost to a community from limiting harvest of marine resources within an MPA can be recovered or exceeded by an associated growth in tourism.[19] In cases where tourism is coupled with an MPA's benefit to adjacent fisheries, increasing the value of the local catch, there is even potential for MPAs to surpass their pre-reserve value.[20] This could lead to a sustainable financing model for at least some MPAs. Other models involve the collection of user or entrance fees from tourists to offset MPA management and program costs.[21] Despite evidence that tourists are willing to pay for access to MPAs where they can enjoy higher quality ocean recreation,[22] however, MPAs in the Caribbean region are still not taking full advantage of this opportunity.[23]

Managing Impacts of Tourism on MPAs

While tourism can help to financially support MPAs, the ecological impacts of tourism can also threaten marine systems within protected areas. Such impacts include water pollution and habitat destruction associated with coastal development and excessive visitor use.[24] As of 2003, there were more than 900 dive operators in the wider Caribbean and an estimated 7.5 million recreational dives in Caribbean MPAs each year.[25] An inexperienced or uncaring diver who breaks off a piece of coral, a boater who damages a reef with a misplaced anchor (Image 4.0.5), or whale watch tours that approach too closely and scare away marine mammals all harm marine systems' health and function while reducing the value of those locations as destinations.

To address visitor impacts, managers can use targeted public outreach programs to help educate visitors and tour operators about best practices and environmentally friendly behaviors. Such efforts rely on appropriate resources to support their implementation. They also require creative approaches in the delivery of positive messages likely to resonate with people in vacation mode, starting with the most basic step of communicating the fact that an MPA exists there. Information can be portrayed on international nautical charts and further identified by marker buoys that indicate sensitive areas. The conservation objectives of an MPA, what led to its designation, and what visitors can do to help support protection goals all need to be communicated in user-friendly ways. Simple outreach efforts like providing MPA brochures at tourism information centers, working with local tourism development councils on messaging, and maintaining an active social media presence can all help build capacity for sustainable tourism in MPAs.

When education and voluntary conservation actions are insufficient and impacts exceed acceptable levels, managers may need to limit access to sensitive habitats. The ability to successfully accommodate and respond to changes in environmental conditions or impacts from tourism is a key component of maintaining MPA effectiveness. To respond to such pressures in the face of climate change, climate-smart ocean tourism in MPAs requires:

- Deliberate integration of climate adaptation programs in MPA management planning.
- Enhanced collaboration with tourism businesses and organizations in joint mitigation and restoration programs.
- Emphasis on ocean tourism best management practices, such as use of marine zoning and implementation of responsible-use certification programs for ocean recreation activities, as a way to increase resilience and reduce visitor use impacts.

Some specific measures that reflect climate-smart tourism planning are described below.

Zoning to Minimize Impacts and Reduce User Conflicts

Marine zoning within MPAs can limit potentially destructive and disruptive activities in sensitive areas and ensure that potentially conflicting uses are spatially separated. Restricting use of motorized personal watercraft in nearshore areas, where they are more likely to disrupt marine wildlife and cause conflict with other recreational users, is one example.[26] A case of marine zoning in practice can be seen in the Florida Keys National Marine Sanctuary (FKNMS). This multiple-use MPA includes zones specifically designed to preserve sensitive areas while allowing some activities compatible with resource protection.

Sanctuary Preservation Areas (SPAs), a type of marine zone found in the FKNMS, restrict consumptive uses in shallow reef areas while allowing nonconsumptive activities like boating, snorkeling, and diving.

Image 4.0.3 Dive boats dot the horizon of Florida Keys National Marine Sanctuary, where mooring buoys provide boaters an alternative to dropping anchor, and help avoid damage to the reef[27]

To better accommodate recreational users while protecting reefs from damage associated with anchoring, the sanctuary placed mooring buoys within these SPAs (Image 4.0.3). These are viewed favorably by user groups like dive operators, most of whom feel these zones have improved diving conditions and reduced conflicts with other user groups, as well as having positive economic impacts for the region.[28]

Responsible Use and Eco-Certification Programs

Eco-certification programs help tourists select operators who meet high sustainable tourism standards. This approach can be incorporated into MPA outreach programs, with managers building partnerships and training tourism operators about responsible environmental practices. In turn, these programs encourage businesses to educate customers about how to avoid harm to the marine environments they are coming to enjoy.[29] One such program developed by the FKNMS is Blue Star, a voluntary recognition and education program that encourages responsible and sustainable diving and snorkeling practices. Tour operators who follow approved guidelines for best practices, maintain staff training, and pass annual reviews by sanctuary staff are certified as Blue Star participants and recognized in sanctuary outreach materials.[30] Blue Star operators further benefit the conservation of the region by serving as frontline educators, helping to reach the more than 700,000 people who snorkel and dive Florida Keys reefs each year.

Partnerships Are Paramount

Impacts of visitors on marine resources are one of the non-climate stressors that MPA managers and tourism practitioners can, and should, partner to address. The sustainable tourism best practices presented in the case studies provide some critical steps for tourism operators and regional development organizations. Additional opportunities lie in partnerships waiting to be developed between MPAs and the tourism industry. Simply practicing sustainable tourism is not enough. Successfully responding to climate change requires further action, like development of coral restoration programs that integrate visitors as volunteers and supporters (see case study 2.1).

Caribbean MPAs, Climate Change, and Tourism

The natural resource and tourism industries of the Caribbean are under threat from the impacts of climate change, compounded by environmental degradation related to overfishing, coastal development, and pollution.[31] In response, a large suite of conservation organizations, national and local governments, and community groups have turned to MPAs to address declines in the health of the region's marine systems. The desire to protect ocean resources both for tourism and local use, further fueled by global marine conservation targets and local communities' stewardship efforts, has led to the creation of over 500 MPAs across 38 countries in the wider Caribbean region as of 2008 (Image 4.0.4).[32] Although reports of MPA coverage vary, recent estimates put the combined total protected area at around 44,400 sq. mi. (115,000 km²), amounting to 4 percent of the wider Caribbean's marine area.[33] A recent study of the insular Caribbean, which includes 25 island governments, identified 376 MPAs that together cover 7.1 percent of the region's marine and coastal areas.[34] The majority of these MPAs are small in size, however, meaning less than 38.6 sq. mi. (100 km²). Designation of larger areas or management of

Image 4.0.4 Distribution of MPAs across the wider Caribbean, as recorded by IUCN and UNEP-WCMC (2013), The World Database on Protected Areas (WDPA), and NOAA Marine Protected Areas Inventory (2014)[35]

dispersed MPAs as cohesive networks could both enhance conservation, but require increased cross-jurisdictional cooperation.

Image 4.0.5 A biologist from Florida Keys National Marine Sanctuary photographs broken elkcorn coral damaged when a boat grounded on the reef[36]

Given the importance of coral reefs to this region and the need to reverse declines in coral reef health, Caribbean MPA managers are increasingly turning to reef restoration as a management practice.[37] The percentage of coral reefs encompassed in Caribbean MPAs rose from 20 percent in 2003 to 30 percent in 2011.[38, 39] Despite this trend, some have concluded that Caribbean coral reefs lack sufficient diversity to be fully resilient.[40] A 2004 analysis of Caribbean MPAs determined that fewer than one in five of those studied were either effective (6 percent) or partially effective (13 percent) at coral reef protection.[41] More recent evaluations of Caribbean MPAs show mixed results with respect to their meeting social and ecological objectives.[42] More work will be needed to further improve the effectiveness of Caribbean MPAs on a regional and local scale.

As tourism in the Caribbean continues to grow, consideration of a potentially unpopular question cannot be overlooked: when and where should tourism *not* be allowed? Protecting the resilience of the region as a whole might require some MPAs to include areas safe from threats associated with tourism, especially if that tourism is not always conducted in a sustainable manner. This more restrictive approach need not always be absolute or permanent, however, and a dynamic approach to zoning may be used to address specific situations. MPA managers and local communities might consider, as an example, restricting access to areas that are demonstrating excessive signs of stress such as during coral bleaching events or an invasive species outbreak.

Conclusion: Linking Tourism and MPA Networks

A coordinated approach to sustainable coastal tourism development and management is essential in an era of climate change. MPA networks can play a key role in such coordination, aiding in information sharing and supporting collaboration to implement best practices in climate-smart conservation. Managers of MPAs can seek training in how to support truly sustainable tourism and achieve effective visitor use management techniques across MPA networks.[43] At the same time, tourism operators can contribute to the stewardship of MPAs by becoming active partners in limiting additional stress to threatened habitats and better educating customers about the importance of protecting these special places.

Connecting regional tourism organizations with MPA groups such as the Caribbean Marine Protected Areas Managers (CaMPAM) network can provide a conduit for linking climate change adaptation strategies between the conservation and tourism sectors. This coordination can help address the innate challenge of managing resources and industries across dozens of countries and cultures within the Caribbean region. The subsequent maintenance of these high-quality destinations through targeted management, education, partnership development, and outreach can allow for responsible and continued visitation along with the associated benefits generated by tourism for coastal communities.

Acknowledgments

A special thanks to Abigail Engleman, Rachel Pawlitz of Florida Keys National Marine Sanctuary, NOAA's National MPA Center, and the Office of National Marine Sanctuaries' Climate Team in compiling supporting information for this piece, and especially Catherine Marzin, Lauren Wenzel, Robert Brock, and Mimi D'Iorio.

Disclaimer

This piece contains conclusions and personal opinions based on accumulated research performed by the original author(s) and does not necessarily reflect the views of NOAA or its Office of National Marine Sanctuaries.

Notes

1. Graeme Kelleher. (1999). *Guidelines for Marine Protected Areas.* Gland, Switzerland and Cambridge, UK: IUCN. Available at: https://portals.iucn.org/library/efiles/documents/PAG-003.pdf.
2. IUCN World Commission on Protected Areas. (2008). *Establishing Marine Protected Area Networks—Making It Happen.* Washington, D.C.: IUCN-WCPA, National Oceanic and Atmospheric Administration and The Nature Conservancy, pp. 118. Available at: http://www.iucn.org/about/work/programmes/marine/marine_our_work/marine_mpas/mpa_publications.cfm?uNewsID=2131.

3. National Marine Protected Areas Center. (2015). *Framework for the National System of Marine Protected Areas of the United States of America.* Silver Spring, MD: National Oceanic and Atmospheric Administration (NOAA). Available at: http://marineprotectedareas .noaa.gov/nationalsystem/framework/final-mpa-framework-0315.pdf.

4. Image Source: Ed Lyman, NOAA National Marine Sanctuaries.

5. IUCN and UNEP-WCMC. (2015). *The World Database on Protected Areas (WDPA).* Cambridge, UK: UNEP- WCMC. Available at: www.protectedplanet.net.

6. Hannah L Thomas, Brian Macsharry, Lance Morgan, Naomi Kingston, Russell Moffitt, Damon Stanwell-Smith, and Louisa Wood. (2014). Evaluating Official Marine Protected Area Coverage for Aichi Target 11. *Aquatic Conservation: Marine and Freshwater Ecosystems,* 42(S2), 8–23. Available at: http://dx.doi.org/10.1002/aqc.2511.

7. Mark Spalding, Imèn Meliane, Amy Milam, Claire Fitzgerald, and Lynne Hale. (2013). Protecting Marine Spaces: Global Targets and Changing Approaches. *Ocean Yearbook Online,* 27(1), 213–248. Available at: http://dx.doi.org/10.1163/22116001-90000160.

8. IUCN. (2014). World Parks Congress Marine Theme. A Strategy of Innovative Approaches and Recommendations to Enhance Implementation of Marine Conservation in the Next Decade. *Promise of Sydney.* Gland, Switzerland: International Union for the Conservation of Nature and Natural Resources. Available at: http:// worldparkscongress.org/downloads/approaches/ThemeM.pdf.

9. Hannah Thomas, et al. (2014). Op cit.

10. Tundi Agardy, Peter Bridgewater, Michael Crosby, Jon Day, Paul Dayton, Richard Kenchington, Dan Laffoley, Patrick McConney, Peter Murray, John Parks, and Lelei Peau. (2003). Dangerous Targets? Unresolved Issues and Ideological Clashes Around Marine Protected Areas. *Aquatic Conservation-Marine and Freshwater Ecosystems,* 13(4), 353–367. Available at: http://dx.doi.org/10.1002/aqc.583.

11. Tundi Agardy, Giuseppe Notarbartolo di Sciara, and Patrick Christie. (2011). Mind the Gap: Addressing the Shortcomings of Marine Protected Areas through Large Scale Marine Spatial Planning. *Marine Policy,* 35(2), 226–232. Available at: http://dx.doi.org/10.1016/ j.marpol.2010.10.006.

12. Image Source: Sean Linnehan, NOAA.

13. Tundi Agardy, Giuseppe Notarbartolo di Sciara, and Patrick Christie. (2011). Op cit.

14. R. Brock, E. Kenchington, and A. Martínez-Arroyo, eds. (2012). *Scientific Guidelines for Designing Resilient Marine Protected Area Networks in a Changing Climate*. Montreal: Commission for Environmental Cooperation. Available at: http://www3.cec.org/islandora/en/item/10820-scientific-guidelines-designing-resilient-marine-protected-area-networks-in-changing-en.pdf.

15. Charles Wahle and Lauren Wenzel. (2013). *A Common Language of Ocean Uses*. Silver Spring, MD: National Oceanic and Atmospheric Administration (NOAA). Available at: http://marineprotectedareas.noaa.gov/pdf/helpful-resources/common_language_ocean_uses_11_14_2013_final.pdf.

16. Edmund Green and Rachel Donnelly. (2003). Recreational Scuba Diving in Caribbean Marine Protected Areas: Do the Users Pay? *AMBIO: A Journal of the Human Environment,* 32(2), 140–144. Available at: http://dx.doi.org/10.1579/0044-7447-32.2.140.

17. Kenneth Broad and James Sanchirico. (2008). Local Perspectives on Marine Reserve Creation in the Bahamas. *Ocean & Coastal Management,* 51(11), 763–771. Available at: http://dx.doi.org/10.1016/j.ocecoaman.2008.07.006.

18. Maureen Hayes, M. Nils Peterson, Justa Heinen-Kay, and R. Brian Langerhans. (2015). Tourism-related Drivers of Support for Protection of Fisheries Resources on Andros Island, The Bahamas. *Ocean & Coastal Management,* 106, 118–123. Available at: http:/dx.doi.org/10.1016/j.ocecoaman.2015.01.007.

19. F. Alban, G. Appéré, and J. Boncoeur. (2008). *Economic Analysis of Marine Protected Areas. A Literature Review*. EMPAFISH Project, Booklet No. 3, pp. 51. Available at: https://www.um.es/empafish/files/Deliverable%205-New%20version.pdf.

20. Enric Sala, Christopher Costello, Dawn Dougherty, Geoffrey Heal, Kieran Kelleher, Jason Murray, Andrew Rosenberg, and Rashid Sumaila. (2013). A General Business Model for Marine Reserves. *PLoS ONE,* 8(4), e58799. Available at: http://dx.doi.org/10.1371/journal.pone.0058799.

21. Steven Thur. (2010). User Fees as Sustainable Financing Mechanisms for Marine Protected Areas: An Application to the Bonaire National Marine Park. *Marine Policy,* 34(1), 63–69. Available at: http://dx .doi.org/10.1016/j.marpol.2009.04.008.

22. Howard Peters and Julie Hawkins. (2009). Access to Marine Parks: A Comparative Study in Willingness to Pay. *Ocean & Coastal Management,* 52(3), 219–228. Available at: http://dx.doi.org/10 .1016/j.ocecoaman.2008.12.001.

23. Edmund Green and Rachel Donnelly. (2003). Op cit.

24. C. Michael Hall. (2001). Trends in Ocean and Coastal Tourism: The End of the Last Frontier? *Ocean & Coastal Management,* 44(9), 601–618.

25. Edmund Green and Rachel Donnelly. (2003). Op cit.

26. Monterey Bay National Marine Sanctuary. (March 5, 2014). *Resource Issues: Motorized Personal Watercraft.* NOAA National Ocean Service. Availabel at: http://montereybay.noaa.gov/resourcepro/resmanissues/mpwc .html.

27. Image Source: Todd Hitchins, NOAA.

28. Manoj Shivlani, Vernon Leeworthy, Thomas Murray, Daniel Suman, and Flavia Tonioli. (2008). Knowledge, Attitudes and Perceptions of Management Strategies and Regulations of the Florida Keys National Marine Sanctuary by Commercial Fishers, Dive Operators, and Environmental Group Members: A Baseline Characterization and 10-year Comparison. *Marine Sanctuaries Conservation Series ONMS-08-06.* Silver Spring, MD: NOAA, pp. 170. Available at: http://sanctuaries.noaa.gov/science/conservation/pdfs/kap2.pdf.

29. NOAA, Office of National Marine Sanctuaries. (in review). *Best Management Practices that Build Capacity for Sustainable Ocean Tourism: Case Studies from the National Marine Sanctuary System.* Training material developed for the International MPA Capacity Building Program, Silver Spring, MD.

30. Florida Keys National Marine Sanctuary. (2015). *Blue Star Program.* Available at: http://floridakeys.noaa.gov/onthewater/bluestar.html.

31. John Knowles, Emma Doyle, Steven Schill, Lynnette Roth, Amy Milam, and George Raber. (2015). Establishing a Marine Conservation Baseline for the Insular Caribbean. *Marine Policy,* 60, 84–97. Available at: http://dx.doi.org/10.1016/j.marpol.2015.05.005.

32. UNEP-WCMC. (2008). *National and Regional Networks of Marine Protected Areas: A Review of Progress.* Cambridge: United Nations Environment Programme, World Conservation Monitoring Centre (UNEP-WCMC). Available at: http://www.unep.org/regionalseas/publications/otherpubs/pdfs/MPA_Network_report.pdf.

33. Lucia Fanning, Robin Mahon, and Patrick McConney. (2013). Applying the Large Marine Ecosystem (LME) Governance Framework in the Wider Caribbean Region. *Marine Policy*, 42, 99–110. Available at: http://dx.doi.org/10.1016/j.marpol.2013.02.008.

34. John Knowles, et al. (2015). Op cit.

35. Image Source: National MPA Center, NOAA.

36. Image Source: NOAA.

37. John Knowles, et al. (2015). Op cit.

38. Lauretta Burke, Jon Maidens, Mark Spalding, Philip Kramer, Edmund Green, Suzie Greenhalgh, Hillary Nobles, and Jonathan Kool. (2004). *Reefs at Risk in the Caribbean.* Washington, DC: World Resources Institute. Available at: http://www.wri.org/publication/reefs-risk-caribbean.

39. Lauretta Burke, Katie Reytar, Mark Spalding, and Allison Perry. (2011). *Reefs at Risk Revisited.* Washington, DC: World Resources Institute, p. 65. Available at: http://www.wri.org/publication/reefs-risk-revisited.

40. Brian Walker and David Salt. (2006). *Resilience Thinking: Sustaining Ecosystems and People in a Changing World.* Washington, D.C.: Island press.

41. Lauretta Burke, et al. (2004). Op cit.

42. Tracey Dalton, Graham Forrester, and Richard Pollnac. (2015). Are Caribbean MPAs Making Progress Toward Their Goals and Objectives? *Marine Policy*, 54, 69–76. Available at: http://dx.doi.org/10.1016/j.marpol.2014.12.009.

43. Thomas Fish and Anne Walton. (2012). Sustainable Tourism Capacity Building for Marine Protected Areas. *PARKS*, 18(2), 108–119. Available at: https://cmsdata.iucn.org/downloads/parks_fish.pdf.

Case Study 4.1

Turneffe Atoll Marine Reserve: Linking Tourism and Conservation in the Face of Climate Change

by Craig Hayes and Kristin Kovalik

Turneffe Atoll, located approximately 30 miles (48 km) east of Belize City, is the largest and most biologically diverse coral atoll in the Caribbean. Considered by many to be the gem of the Mesoamerican Reef System, the atoll encompasses nearly all coastal-marine ecosystems in a relatively isolated area. Its healthy reefs are a major attraction for scuba divers. The expansive back reef flats on the eastern side of the atoll provide habitat for bonefish and permit, which are key species for Turneffe's economically important sport fishing industry. Turneffe Atoll is also an important commercial fishery with the primary target species being Caribbean spiny lobster, queen conch, and finfish.

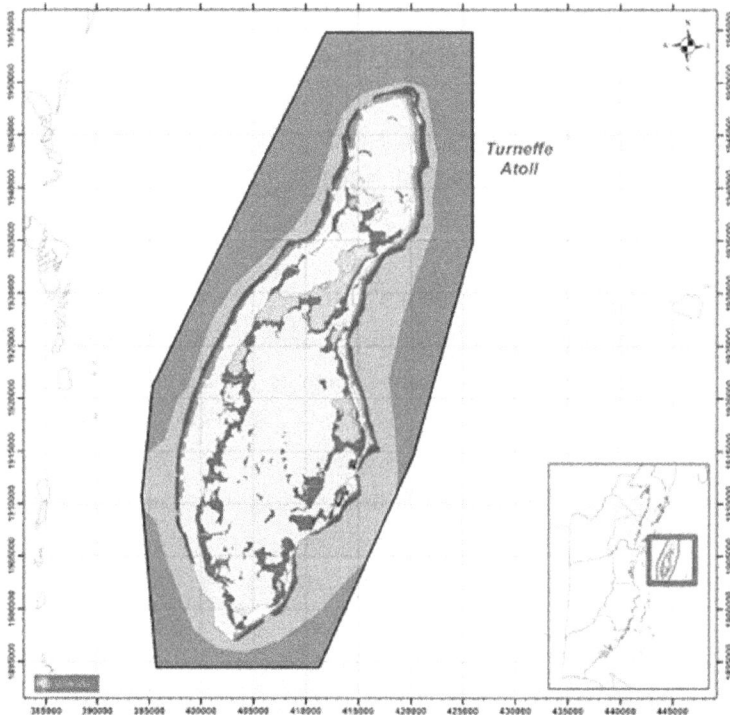

4.1.1 Map of Turneffe Atoll[1]

Development and Increased Threats
from Climate Change

Much of Turneffe Atoll is low-lying swampy terrain, and threats related to climate change and sea level rise are high. Although it is difficult to quantify changes purely related to climate change, we are seeing more pronounced beach erosion, possibly due to a rise in sea level. In recent years there have also been large influxes of sargassum seaweed, possibly due in part to ocean warming or a change in currents (see case study 2.1.3). Other changes, such as coral bleaching, are likely related to a combination of environmental factors including warming.

Turneffe Atoll contains the most extensive mangrove coverage found on Belize's cays.[2] Mangroves are among the most valuable ecosystems in the world.[3] They are a known carbon sink and provide coastal protection from storms, flood control, natural water purification, and fish habitat. Turneffe Atoll plays a significant role in protecting the Belize mainland, and particularly Belize City, from storms. The annualized value of storm protection and damage avoided by Turneffe Atoll is estimated at US $38 million.[4]

Image 4.1.2 Grassy Caye Range. Turneffe Atoll is made up of nearly 20 individual cayes (or cays), many of which are covered with dense mangroves that provide critical habitat as well as storm protection[5]

Since 2000, the transfer of property on Turneffe Atoll from national to private ownership has skyrocketed, resulting in increased development pressure. Already this has led to some destructive development that could exacerbate the effects of climate change in the future. The most ominous practice involves clearing mangroves, which are then filled by dredging critically important marine habitats such as seagrasses and backreef flats. Impacts related to these practices include increased erosion, loss of natural protection from storm damage, loss of carbon sink effects, direct damage to coral reefs, and beach erosion.

The Turneffe Atoll Marine Reserve

Due largely to Turneffe Atoll's ecological and socioeconomic importance to Belize, stakeholders including the Government of Belize and Belizean conservation organizations have worked for the past 25 years to establish guidelines for sustainably managing the atoll. For much of this time, however, these efforts produced little more than a stack of documents on a government shelf. In 2010, Turneffe Atoll Trust, a nonprofit organization developed by the owners of Turneffe Flats Resort, formed a coalition of parties interested in protecting the atoll. This group's efforts led in 2012 to the creation of the Turneffe Atoll Marine Reserve (TAMR), which at 325,412 acres (131,690 ha) is Belize's largest marine reserve.

Establishing the Turneffe Atoll Marine Reserve involved over 10,000 person-hours of consultation among stakeholders. Commercial fishermen in Belize have traditionally opposed marine reserves and other fisheries management interventions, largely due to concern that reserves only limit their fishing rights and negatively affect their livelihoods. Initially, the commercial fishermen at Turneffe were strongly opposed to a marine reserve. Over the year-long consultative process, however, they came to understand the need for and potential benefits of the reserve. In the end, fairly broad-based support developed among the fishermen, based partly on guarantees that they would be involved with management of the reserve.

From the beginning, the top priority for the commercial fishing sector has been improved fisheries enforcement. No-take zones have been established and marked; approximately 15 percent of the reserve is now off limits to all fishing aside from catch-and-release sport fishing. An essential part of this effort was fostering closer working relationships among key stakeholder groups at Turneffe, particularly the commercial fishing and ecotourism sectors.

A stakeholder group, the Turneffe Atoll Sustainability Association (TASA), was organized to oversee the marine reserve with all key stakeholders having board-level representation. TASA co-manages the reserve along with the Belize Fisheries Department and guarantees board positions to the commercial fishing and tourism sectors, the University of Belize, private landowners, conservation leaders, scientists, and the Turneffe Atoll Trust. While TASA is focused on monitoring and enforcement of the reserve, Turneffe Atoll Trust is committed to long-term protection of the atoll through land acquisition and conservation. Turneffe Flats Resort plays a significant role within both of these organizations.

The plan is for the reserve to establish management fees that will generate revenue for operations. Most funding, however, will likely come from private donations. The Turneffe Atoll Marine Reserve is very fortunate to have received a major donation from the Bertarelli Foundation, which funds marine conservation and life science projects.[6] Fundraising will be an

Image 4.1.3 Aerial view of Turneffe Flats Lodge[7]

ongoing focus for the reserve, but the generous donation from the Bertarelli Foundation has made it possible to begin full operations. Permanent reserve headquarters are awaiting government approval but will begin construction in the near future. Community-building efforts have been ongoing as well.

The Role of the Tourism Sector
in Addressing Climate Change

The ecotourism sector, particularly Turneffe Flats Resort, has been a driving force for conservation efforts at Turneffe, including development of the marine reserve. Turneffe Atoll Trust was initially established by Turneffe Flats Resort to address the ecological challenges of Turneffe Atoll and other coastal marine areas. The Trust funded the creation of the Turneffe Atoll Marine Reserve Management Plan, required to establish the TAMR. Turneffe Flats Resort has also provided accommodations, food, dockage, and fuel for full-time enforcement teams, leading to improved enforcement of fisheries regulations as well as more support from fishermen.

The Turneffe Atoll Marine Reserve Management Plan[8] provides much of the framework for addressing climate change issues for Turneffe Atoll. The plan details the mission, objectives, and strategies for the TAMR, addresses threats to the atoll, and develops a framework for managing the resources of Turneffe Atoll while promoting its important socioeconomic benefits, including sustainable commercial fishing and the development of high-value, low-impact tourism.

Conclusion

The Turneffe Atoll Marine Reserve is still in its infancy. There is much to be done, and successful adaptation to climate change will require continued stakeholder involvement, education, cooperation between NGOs and government agencies, and ongoing financial support. Nonetheless, we believe the successes we have achieved to date show that marine reserves can play an important part in responding to threats like climate change. They can also be a critical part of sustainable tourism plans for Caribbean islands and coastal nations. We hope that Turneffe Atoll can be a model for others in the region seeking to balance tourism with environmental protection and a concerted response to climate change.

Notes

1. Image Source: Wildtracks.
2. Coastal Zone Management Authority and Institute. (2015). *Turneffe Atoll Coastal Zone Management Guidelines*. Belize Integrated Coastal Zone Management Plan. Belize City: CZMAI. Available at: http://www.coastalzonebelize.org/wp-content/uploads/2015/08/Turneffe-Atoll-Coastal-Zone-Management-Guidelines.pdf.
3. Mark Spalding, Anna McIvor, Femke Tonneijck, Susanna Tol, and Pieter van Eijk. (2014). *Mangroves for Coastal Defence: Guidelines for Coastal Managers and Policy Makers*. Wetlands International and The Nature Conservancy. Available at: http://www.nature.org/media/oceansandcoasts/mangroves-for-coastal-defence.pdf.
4. Anthony Fedler. (2011). *The Economic Value of Turneffe Atoll: Full Report*. Prepared for the Turneffe Atoll Trust by Human Dimensions Consulting. Available at: http://www.turneffeatoll.org/app/webroot/userfiles/66/File/Turneffe%20Atoll%20Valuation.pdf.
5. Image Source: Turneffe Atoll Trust.
6. Fondation Bertarelli. (2016). *About*. Available at: http://www.fondation-bertarelli.org/about/.
7. Image Source: Turneffe Atoll Trust.
8. Belize Fisheries Department. (2012). *Turneffe Atoll Marine Reserve Management Plan, 2012-2017*. Belize City, Belize. Available at: http://www.turneffeatollmarinereserve.org/app/webroot/userfiles/214/File/Final%20Turneffe%20Atoll%20Management%20Plan%2014%2009%202012%20Fisheries%20Edited.pdf

Case Study 4.2

Jardines de la Reina: The Crown Jewel of Cuban MPAs[1]

by Daria Siciliano

Background

The ecologically rich and relatively understudied Cuban coasts have not experienced the levels of development seen in the rest of the Caribbean. This is due in large part to the U.S. trade embargo of the country, which dates back to the early 1960s. Although the countries are divided by just 100 miles (160 km) of water, there has been very little trade or travel between them for the past 55 years. The embargo has also greatly limited scientific collaboration. While American scientists have been allowed to travel to Cuba under specific research licenses issued by the U.S. Department of the Treasury, by early 2014 only a handful of American universities and NGOs had established collaborations with Cuban peers. This was typically accomplished in spite of severe resource limitations and vexing bureaucratic challenges on both sides.

On December 17th, 2014, U.S. President Barack Obama ordered the restoration of full diplomatic relations with Cuba and the opening of a U.S. embassy in Havana for the first time in more than half a century. While the president's order did not actually lift the embargo, it broke an enduring stalemate between two countries and represented a turning point—one largely embraced by the scientific, research, environmental, and medical communities in the U.S. and Cuba. There are some cautions to that endorsement, however. Many scientists and resource managers believe that the U.S. embargo of Cuba has been a double-edged sword for the Caribbean nation. While it has certainly limited economic, social, and cultural contacts between the two nations, it has also indirectly helped to protect Cuba's diverse ecosystems.

Consider tourism as an example. Cuba, roughly the size of the U.S. state of Florida, hosts only 3 million tourists per year, generating about US $76 million in direct revenue.[2] Florida, in contrast, hosts upwards of 90 million tourists annually, generating more than US $65 billion in revenue. Before the 1959 Cuban Revolution, 90 percent of its tourism market was from the United States.[3] If and when the embargo is eventually lifted, Cuba will likely experience a boom in American tourism. The relaxed travel restrictions recently enacted have already resulted in a surge in visitation starting in 2015 from qualifying American travelers.[4]

The embargo has also had a major impact on fishing, farming, energy, and other resource industries. Cuba has been prevented from exporting its fisheries resources to the U.S. market, for example, and its 300 million potential consumers. Meanwhile, its agricultural sector tends to be based on small-scale, organic farming. Without the pressure of large-scale commercial fishing and farming to support U.S. demand, Cuba has managed to protect its natural resources while reducing environmental impacts such as overfishing and the widespread use of chemical fertilizers and pesticides. These factors have helped preserve the integrity of the island's coastal and marine ecosystems.[5]

The Cuban government has also historically taken a progressive stance in crafting environmental legislation and managing its natural resources, especially its marine assets. The Cuban government's current goal is to include 25 percent of the insular shelf in marine protected areas.[6] The 108 MPAs in Cuban waters catalogued in 2004 already cover 15 percent of Cuba's insular shelf, 35 percent of its coral reefs, 31 percent of its seagrass beds, 27 percent of its mangroves, and 16 fish spawning sites. Of these MPAs, 48 have national relevance and the remaining 59 areas have local significance.[7] This case study examines the largest of these MPAs, Jardines de la Reina (Gardens of the Queen).

An Effective Cuban MPA

The Jardines de la Reina archipelago stretches 224 miles (360 km) in length and lies about 62 miles (100 km) south of the central Cuban coast. It is composed of more than 650 uninhabited cays and includes a variety of coral reef, seagrass, and mangrove systems. In 1996, the Cuban government set aside 367 sq. mi. (950 km^2) of the archipelago as a no-take zone, naming it the Jardines de la Reina (Gardens of the Queen) Marine Reserve—the largest MPA in the Caribbean. There is limited recreational access to the site; only 1,000 divers and 500 catch-and-release fishermen are permitted to enter the MPA each year.

To measure the effectiveness of the Jardines de la Reina MPA, researchers from Cuba's Center for Coastal Ecosystems studied densities of the 10 most frequent, highly targeted, and relatively large reef fish species inside and outside the reserve over a period of a year and a half.[8] They found higher abundance inside the reserve for most months, with 5 out of the 10 species twice as plentiful inside the reserve. Previous studies had found that ecological conditions were similar inside and outside the reserve, while fishing pressures prior to reserve designation were also similar. In light of these factors, the differences in species abundance could be explained only by the effective protection inside the reserve. Additional anecdotal evidence comes from scientists and tourists who have visited this jewel of a marine reserve. The reserve has large numbers of huge groupers, snappers, and sharks in addition to healthy coral stands and large mangroves, all of which have largely disappeared elsewhere in the Caribbean.

Image 4.2.1 A black grouper cruises a reef in the Jardines de la Reina Marine Reserve. Black groupers are a commercially valuable species that can reach lengths up to 5 feet (150 cm) and can weigh over 200 pounds (90 kg)[9]

Role of Tourism in Jardines de la Reina

Recognizing that the main attraction of the reserve is its unspoiled natural riches, tourist operations play a pivotal role in the protection of the MPA. The income and public interest generated through tourism contribute significantly to scientific monitoring and research, conservation, and enforcement. Tourist operations in Jardines de la Reina are carefully managed through a private-public partnership between the government agency Marlin Marinas and AVALON, a private company with Italian ownership that was involved in the national park establishment over 20 years ago, and has been managing ecotourism operations there ever since. The most important international market since 2012 has been Europeans, accounting for 90 percent of visitors, with the remaining 10 percent from North America. The most important countries by numbers of visitors are, in order, Russia, the Czech Republic, Italy, the United Kingdom, Canada, and Spain.

The initial market in Jardines de la Reina focused on recreational diving, which brought the reserve to the attention of international visitors. According to the 2012–2016 Jardines de la Reina Management Plan,[10] the

Image 4.2.2 The floating Tortuga Hotel at Cayo Anclitas[11]

MPA now averages 800 visitors per year, 51 percent of whom are recreational divers. Diving has been surpassed in economic importance by sport fishing, however, due to the higher revenues this activity generates. Most visitors stay at the Hotel Tortuga, a floating barge in Anclitas, the main cay located in the middle of the archipelago. The hotel has 7 private rooms and maintains 6 yachts, including 4 live-aboards, and 23 support boats.

Climate Change and Current Threats to Jardines de la Reina

The principal threats to the Jardines de la Reina ecosystem include loss of two key habitats, mangroves and reef crest, particularly its elkhorn coral (*Acropora palmata*) gardens. Both losses are related to climate change. While the proximal reasons for mangrove die offs are still under investigation, they have been linked to more intense and frequent extreme meteorological events, likely connected to the warming climate. The loss of *A. palmata* is also directly related to climate change since one of the main culprits appears to be increased bleaching, a phenomenon that occurs during times of stress (including thermal stress) when corals expel their symbiotic algae, causing them to appear white.[12]

Coral bleaching events in the Caribbean have increased both in frequency and extent, and this is attributed at least in part to rising ocean temperatures in this region. The higher resilience found in healthy reefs such as those in Jardines de la Reina may help with long-term mitigation of climate change effects. This resilience might eventually prove to be a double-edged sword, however. As the Jardines de la Reina ecosystem fares better in the face of a changing climate than other Caribbean reefs, this might drive increased visitation and tourism activities such as recreational diving and fishing.

Illegal fishing also remains a threat. After designation of the reserve, commercial fishing efforts relocated outside of it. As with any large marine reserve, however, particularly those in developing nations, enforcement presents a challenge. Due to the site's limited budget, most of the MPA's enforcement activities are concentrated in its central area where a research station also exists. Some poaching of large, commercially valuable species has been observed along the edges of the reserve.

A Future of Protecting Shared Resources

Marine organisms have always flowed freely between Cuba and the U.S., depending on healthy habitats on both sides of the Florida Straits and paying no heed to international boundaries or economic embargoes. Reflecting this open border, Cuban and American scientists and resource managers recognize the need to develop common scientific understandings and policies to protect our shared marine resources. The recent political thaw between the two countries, and the new U.S. policy toward Cuba, are hopeful steps in the right direction.

On November 18, 2015, the U.S. National Oceanic and Atmospheric Administration and the U.S. National Park Service signed a historic memorandum of understanding with Cuba's Ministry of Science, Technology and Environment and its Center for Protected Areas to cooperate on the conservation and management of marine protected areas. This MOU represents one of the first bilateral arrangements following the recent renewal of diplomatic relations. Jardines de la Reina is a successfully designed and implemented MPA, and represents a model for what the U.S. and Cuba

Image 4.2.3 Northern Cay in the Jardines de la Reina archipelago[13]

can achieve in joint management of shared resources once the embargo is lifted and the countries' scientists and conservationists can work together in earnest.

At the same time, thawing relations means a likely boom in American-driven tourism that could undo years of careful management of Cuba's marine resources. It is essential that foresight and careful planning precede the coming tide of development and tourism, which carry with them possibly disastrous environmental consequences. Bilateral protections must be established before changes in U.S. travel restrictions result in an enormous wave of tourism, causing dramatically increased beach visitation, boat traffic, fishing, and coastal development, all of which will threaten Cuba's precious and fragile marine ecosystems. We will not get a second chance.

Notes

1. An earlier, shorter version of this paper appeared as: Daria Siciliano. (2015). Perspective: The MPAs of Cuba and the implications of a potential end to the US embargo. *MPA News,* 16(3). Available at: http://depts.washington.edu/mpanews/MPA141.htm.
2. WTTC. (2015). *Travel & Tourism Economic Impact 2015: Cuba.* London: World Travel & Tourism Council.
3. Kenyon Lindeman, James Tripp, Daniel Whittle, Azur Moulaert-Quiros, and Emma Stewart. (2003). Sustainable Coastal Tourism in Cuba: Roles of Environmental Assessments, Certification Programs, and Protection Fees. *Tulane Environmental Law Journal,* 16(special issue), 533–589. Available at: http://www.lexisnexis.com.prxy4.ursus .maine.edu/lnacui2api/api/version1/getDocCui?lni=4969-F1Y0 -00CV-S0G8&csi=139128&hl=t&hv=t&hnsd=f&hns=t&hgn=t& oc=00240&perma=true.
4. Associated Press in Havana. (2015). US travel to Cuba surges 36% following thaw in diplomatic relations. *The Guardian,* May 26, 2015. Available at: http://www.theguardian.com/world/2015/may/ 26/us-american-cuba-travel-tourism-increase.
5. Claudia Adrien. (2015). In a post-embargo era, Cuba serves as a model for marine protection. *Deutsche Welle.* Available at:

http://www.dw.com/en/in-a-post-embargo-era-cuba-serves-as-a-model-for-marine-protection/a-18475940.

6. A. José Areces, J. Gerhartz, R. Duttit, and C. Martínez. (2012). *Assessing Representativeness of the Cuban Subsystem of Marine Protected Areas (SMPA), I: An Overview.* Scientific Submission to the Wider Caribbean and Western Mid-Atlantic Regional Workshop to Facilitate the Description of Ecologically or Biologically Significant Marine Areas. Recife, Brazil, 28 February–2 March 2012. UNEP Convention on Biological Diversity. Available at: https://www.cbd.int/doc/meetings/mar/rwebsa-wcar-01/official/rwebsa-wcar-01-sbstta-16-inf-07-en.pdf.

7. Reinaldo Estrada Estrada, Aylem Hernández Avila, José Luis Gerhartz Muro, Augusto Martínez Zorrilla, Marvel Melero Leon, Michel Bliemsrieder Izquierdo, and Kenyon C. Lindeman. (2004). *The National System of Marine Protected Areas in Cuba.* Ciudad Habana, Cuba: National Center for Protected Areas (CNAP). Available at: http://cos.fit.edu/education/documents/New_Folder/2004%20 Cuban%20MPA%20System.pdf.

8. Fabián Pina-Amargós, Gaspar González-Sansón, Félix Martín-Blanco, and Abel Valdivia. (2014). Evidence for Protection of Targeted Reef Fish on the Largest Marine Reserve in the Caribbean. *PeerJ* 2:e274. Available at: https://doi.org/10.7717/peerj.274.

9. Image Source: Noel Lopez.

10. Ministerio de la Agricultura, Empresa nacional Para la Proteccion de la Flora y la Fauna. (2012). *Plan De Manejo Parque Nacional Jardines de la Reina, 2012-2016.* Ciego de Avila/Camaguey.

11. Image Source: Fernando Bretos.

12. National Ocean Service. (2015). *What is Coral Bleaching?* National Ocean and Atmospheric Administration (NOAA), U.S. Department of Commerce. Available at: http://oceanservice.noaa.gov/facts/coral_bleach.html.

13. Image Source: Daria Siciliano.

Case Study 4.3

Cabo Pulmo, Baja California, Mexico: Linking Community Resilience with Marine Conservation

by Martin Goebel, Carlos Godinez-Reyes,
Sula Vanderplank and Judith Castro Lucero

No place on Earth is immune to environmental change, including a warming planet. But some places provide hope that ecological decline can be reversed and the specter of climate change can be mitigated, especially when communities of place and communities of purpose work together with common goals. This is the case of Cabo Pulmo in Baja California Sur, Mexico. In this case study, we describe how Cabo Pulmo, a small, organically developing coastal community, might be a resilient model for dealing with the consequences of change, including those brought by climate trends and extreme weather events. An important part of this story is the Cabo Pulmo National Park (CPNP).

Image 4.3.1 Cabo Pulmo's pristine beaches, relatively undeveloped coastline, and coral reefs attract visitors from around the world[1]

The Context

Cabo Pulmo is literally off the beaten track, reached by 6 miles (10 km) of dirt road. It is located just south of the town of La Ribera on the central East Cape of the Sea of Cortez, about 60 miles (100 km) north of Cabo San Lucas and a 1.5-hour drive from the San Jose del Cabo International Airport. The village numbers roughly 120 to 150 people. Quite literally, everyone knows everyone. In a region increasingly affected by change, this has been an advantage. Due to its proximity to the U.S. border, in the past 20 years a small retiree community of mostly American expatriates has also gravitated to this rustic, undeveloped, isolated oasis full of natural beauty and bounty.

Most residents have thatched roofed casita-style homes and rentals. While there are six restaurants, Cabo Pulmo has just one tiny grocery store and no paved streets. It is not connected to any electrical grid. Instead, the village and homes are powered mostly by solar panels and small diesel engines. This lack of development has actually proven an advantage in terms of resilience. In 2014, for example, despite Hurricane Odile's devastating impacts in the region, Cabo Pulmo suffered very little. There were no prolonged power outages and only a few structures were seriously damaged.

The Castros, a multi-generational Mexican family that first settled here in the 1890s, comprise a majority of local residents. Once very prosperous pearl divers and fishers, the Castro family embraced change beginning in the early 1990s. Their motivation was not a changing climate, however. Instead, it was a shift in economic activity brought by the confluence of three forces: declining fishing success, growing public appreciation for coral reefs and marine environments, and increasing visitation, mainly by divers. With help from the professors, researchers, and students at the Autonomous University of Baja California Sur, the Castros and the village of Cabo Pulmo made the difficult choice to shift from fishing to nature-based tourism and conservation as the source of their future livelihood.

Creating and Managing the Cabo Pulmo National Park

Cabo Pulmo's main attraction is its naturalness, especially the nearby Cabo Pulmo Reef, the northernmost reef system on the Pacific coast of North America. According to a 2011 letter sent to the Director of UNESCO's World Heritage Center by 22 prominent marine scientists, Cabo Pulmo "may be the oldest and most important reef in the American Pacific." As they explain:

> Comprised of 25 different species of corals, the reef supports a rich diversity of species, including 154 species of marine invertebrates and 226 species of fish. Its inhabitants and visitors include humpback and Bryde's whales, tiger sharks, three types of dolphins, manta rays, marlins, tuna and five of the world's seven endangered species of sea turtles.[2]

This biological richness was threatened in the latter half of the 20th century as sport fishers and commercial fishers decimated local fish populations. Concerned for the future of their reefs and livelihoods, local communities pressured the government to declare the region off-limits to fishing.

In 1995, with support from the state government of Baja California Sur and the National Institute of Ecology (INE), the marine area adjacent to Cabo Pulmo was declared a federal Natural Protected Area, with severe

Image 4.3.2 Meetings of local residents helped build and maintain support for the creation of the Cabo Pulmo National Park[3]

restrictions on fishing and other resource extraction. In 2000, the site, which includes 17,570 acres (7,111 hectares) containing the Cabo Pulmo Reef, was renamed as Cabo Pulmo National Park.[4] Portions of the adjacent coastline are protected as a Terrestrial Federal Marine Zone.[5] International designations followed: in 2005 the area was made a UNESCO World Heritage Site, part of the "Islands and Protected Areas of the Gulf of California," and in 2008 Cabo Pulmo was named a "wetland of particular importance" under the Ramsar Convention.[6]

Scientific monitoring has shown that biodiversity is growing in the park, with fish biomass in the park increasing by over 460 percent between 1999 and 2009 alone.[7] In the same time period, the biomass of top predators such as groupers increased by 11 times.[8] This has been made possible by a stringent no-take policy that has been effectively enforced by local residents, who recognize the value that ecotourism and conservation of marine resources can provide over the long term. As Aburto-Oropeza et al. (2011) conclude, "The success of CPNP is greatly due to local leadership, effective self-enforcement by local stakeholders, and the general support of the broader community."[9]

The Growth of Marine Tourism

While today the Cabo Pulmo National Park is recognized as among the best examples of reef recovery worldwide, the early years were difficult. Fish and reef health had been affected by years of uncontrolled fishing. As national park managers[10] placed restrictions on resource use, tensions over sovereignty and authority were inevitable. Meanwhile, residents of Cabo Pulmo had little experience and capacity to manage and promote the kind of tourism a national park could foster. Local incomes plummeted for a number of years, even while foreigners trickled in, bought, and built. Discomfort grew among local residents. The Castro family wondered if they had made the right choices.

Eventually the tide turned, however, as word spread of the park's existence and the increasing biodiversity of the reefs. Dive operations developed, science demonstrated that fish and reef recovery were on the rise, and tourist visitation slowly began to improve the economy. The promise of a better future began to emerge. Today, Cabo Pulmo

Image 4.3.3 A spectacular school of jacks surrounds a diver near Cabo Pulmo. Such prolific marine life, the result of careful protection by local residents and others, attracts thousands of divers to this area every year[11]

is a popular and growing destination for divers and other outdoor enthusiasts. New opportunities have been developed, including lodging, camping, kayaking, hiking, biking, birdwatching, and sport fishing (outside the park boundary). Cabo Pulmo now attracts people from near and far. A number of small businesses are becoming more and more successful and sustainable. Yet Cabo Pulmo remains small, basic, and rustic. Indeed, that is at the core of the place's endearing charm.

Cabo Pulmo's location on one of northwest Mexico's most picturesque coasts, and its success as an internationally significant marine conservation site, has catapulted it into the national and global spotlight. Numerous scientific articles, news stories, films, and documentaries have helped to spread the word. It seems everyone now wants to be part of this success story. And that has led to new challenges and threats.

The Paradox of Success

At one time, Mexico's northwest region was remote and undeveloped. But today, southern Baja's accessibility to American and Canadian tourist markets—along with Mexico's aggressive tourism investment and promotion policies, which are especially favorable to large-scale developments—have conspired to attract investors of all stripes along both the East Cape and Western Pacific coasts. As a result, once isolated coastal corridors are spurring much speculative investment and there is a gold rush of medium- and large-scale projects with dubious probabilities of sustainable success.

Around Cabo Pulmo much land is for sale, most of it in large blocks. At least 18 development projects are either permitted or proposed in the zone between Los Barriles/Buenavista and Vinorama. Many of these have pitted marine and terrestrial biodiversity conservationists, scientists, and community leaders against conventional large resort developers and pro-development politicians. In very public and contentious ways, mega-development projects like "Cabo Cortez" and "Cabo Dorado" have catalyzed advocacy efforts in favor of a conservation-based development vision.

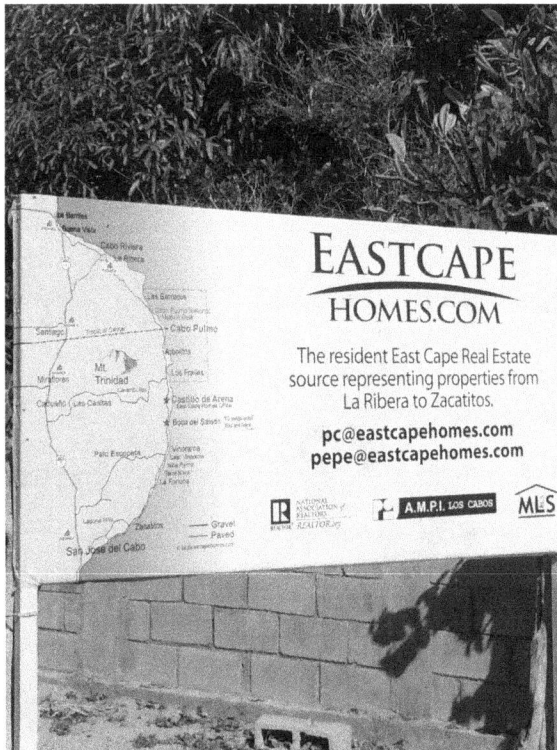

Image 4.3.4 Just one of many signs advertising new development projects in the region[12]

Thus far, social cohesion in Cabo Pulmo and its alliances with outside organizations have successfully fended off the most destructive projects. Scientists, Mexico's Parks Commission, and environmental and community advocates have worked in relative concert to achieve common goals. Two local nonprofit organizations and several regional, national, and international conservation groups, universities, and philanthropies have created a strong coalition committed to Cabo Pulmo's long-term sustainability. Nonetheless, the threat from overdevelopment continues, and it is now compounded by the risks created by a rapidly changing climate.

Climate Change: A Looming Threat

There is little doubt the climate is changing in the Sea of Cortez region. This is normally a dry, water-stressed region where aquifers recharge slowly. Today, increasing dry periods are cause for concern, especially when the region's population and demands for water are growing. (This is certainly the case for the La Paz and Los Cabos regions of southern Baja. With 8.5 percent annual population growth, Los Cabos is the fastest

Image 4.3.5 Massive amounts of silt and sand are being deposited at the mouths of arroyos including Arroyo Santiago (above), near La Ribera[13]

growing population center in Mexico.) The Baja California peninsula seems to be undergoing drought years followed by abnormally wet periods. Over the last few years, rains and storms, including hurricanes, have begun as early as June when historically they began in August or September. Early rains and stronger storms have also caused arroyos (seasonally dry river beds) to surge with torrential runoff making its way from the mountains to the ocean. This has caused serious destruction to settlements in and near these arroyos.

These changes are already affecting the region's tourism industry. In September 2014, Hurricane Odile, among the strongest on record to hit the tip of Baja California, caused catastrophic damage and shut down the international airport for over 1 month. Many hotels and resorts were unable to operate for several months. New projects under construction have also been affected. One example is the Cabo Riviera marina and resort, located just north of Cabo Pulmo in the town of La Ribera. Situated at the southern end of the mouth of Arroyo Santiago, Cabo Riviera has been plagued by work stoppages as a result of massive amounts of water and sand flooding the marina and development.

Cabo Pulmo itself is experiencing climate change impacts. Most evident are those in the village of Cabo Pulmo and within the coastal zone of the Cabo Pulmo National Park. One challenge is the encroachment of high tides into the federal maritime zone, known as a ZOFEMAT (Zona Federal Marítima Terrestre). This zone is reserved for public access and extends from the shore to a line 20 meters inland from the high tide mark. Because of sea level rise and changes in shorelines, this zone is in a state of flux, leading to jurisdictional and management conflicts. Some homes and sea walls, for example, now lie within the ZOFEMAT. Meanwhile, new rock and concrete barriers are being constructed in this zone in response to rising sea levels. Unfortunately, these are deflecting energy to surrounding beaches, causing erosion.

In the main park visitor area, which includes parking lots, a restaurant, and recreation businesses, the beach is gradually disappearing. In the Las Barracas sector of the park, where beaches and dunes are being lost, a number of homes have been severely affected and some destroyed due to strong tide and wave action. Moreover, the beach and dune area at Las Barracas, designated as an active sea turtle nesting site, is shrinking

Image 4.3.6 Encroachment of the sea as well as lax building practices has led to scenes like this one, with homes and seawalls crumbling into the ocean[14]

quickly. In addition, annual reef surveys indicate the early onset of coral bleaching. Both reefs and turtles are important to the conservation mission of the park and to its visitors; their decline could have a deleterious effect on both.

Just north of Cabo Pulmo lies Punta Arena, home to some very specialized habitats that have formed over millennia.[15] These complex dune systems formed from repeated deposition from Arroyo Santiago, which eventually stopped the small arroyo from reaching the sea. Seasonal lagoons form behind the dunes when rains wash down from the highlands and pool on the silty soils. The lagoons are home to species found nowhere else in the world such as *Pisonia calafia* (*Nyctaginaceae*), a spiny tree with fewer than 30 known individuals in the world.[16] Changes in the conditions that created these unique species could drive some to extinction.

Climate Change and Future Challenges

The current management plan for Cabo Pulmo, published in 2009, does not address climate change per se.[17] However, management authorities (including the coauthors of this case study) are currently updating the plan. As a first step, coastal dynamics experts from the Center for Scientific Research and Higher Education at Ensenada (CICESE), a regional oceanographic research institute, have been engaged to help understand the changes and forecast probable coastal dynamics scenarios. Over the coming years, management priorities in an era of climate change include:

- Creating a terrestrial buffer around Cabo Pulmo National Park, including possible acquisition of key lands around the park.
- Ensuring that coastal development considers the spectrum of direct and indirect impacts to marine and coastal ecosystems.
- Adopting adaptation and mitigation measures inside and outside the park zone, especially for buildings and structures in the dunes and coastal zone.
- Ensuring efficient use of water and equitable access to it, as well as the integrity of arroyos and critical aquifer recharge areas. Access to water will undoubtedly be a contentious issue as population grows on the East Cape and in Los Cabos.

Conclusion: Commitment, Recovery, and Prosperity

Few visitors leave Cabo Pulmo without learning its unusual, uplifting story, grounded in the community's unwavering commitment to the recovery and protection of nature. Its place in the annals of conservation history is already assured and celebrated worldwide. It is a UNESCO World Heritage Site and a Ramsar Convention wetland of particular importance. The Natural Resources Defense Council has bestowed Cabo Pulmo with its "BioGem" designation. And globally known conservation leader Dr. Sylvia Earle has called Cabo Pulmo the "jewel in the crown" of the Gulf of California and a "Mission Blue Hope Spot," saying that diving there today "is almost like diving into the ocean as it was 50 years ago."[18]

Cabo Pulmo has confronted and adapted to profound change. Its residents and a growing cadre of recurring visitors, dedicated scientists, and loyal supporters make for an unusually strong alliance. Collectively, they share a clear commitment to science and a conservation-based future. Based on the three pillars of shared purpose, knowledge, and strong relationships, they create the social infrastructure and social capital vital to overcoming challenges.

Cabo Pulmo is an evolving narrative. But already it has demonstrated several important tenets. The first is that, if protected, a marine ecosystem can sometimes recover rapidly. The second is that scientific research is important in revealing profound issues, like water scarcity and the impacts of arroyo and dune development, implicit in large-scale tourism and other types of development. The third is that a motivated and informed local community, backed by regional and international allies, can stave off and hopefully turn away conventional, large-scale coastal development and create more sustainable alternative development models. Ultimately, Cabo Pulmo demonstrates that it is possible to survive, indeed flourish, when stewardship is chosen over resource extraction and rapid development, especially when unpredictable change looms.

Notes

1. Image Source: Ralph Lee Hopkins.
2. Exequiel Ezcurra, Octavio Aburto-Oropeza, Sylvia Earle, Daniel Pauly, Enric Sala, Nancy Knowlton, Robert Warner, Mark Hixon, Rick Starr, Edith Widder, Camilo Mora, James Ketchum, Armando Trasviña-Castro, Horacio Perez España, Eduardo F. Balart, Micheline Cariño, Rafael Riosmena-Rodríguez, Oscar Arizpe, Hector Reyes Bonilla, Carlos Sánchez Ortiz, Andres Lopez Perez, and Jorge Cortés. (2011). Letter to Mr. Kishore Rao, Director, UNESCO World Heritage Centre, *Re: The Protected Area of Cabo Pulmo National Park, in Baja California Sur, Mexico.* May 23, 2011. Available at: http://docplayer.net/13098443-Re-the-protected-area-of-cabo-pulmo-national-park-in-baja-california-sur-mexico.html.
3. Image Source: Carlos Aguilera.
4. Cabo Pulmo Vivo and Amigos para la Conservación de Cabo Pulmo, A.C. (2009). *Report of Tourist's Real Estate Projects and its*

Potencial [sic] Impacts in the Ramsar Site of Cabo Pulmo. Available at: http://www.aida-americas.org/sites/default/files/refDocuments/Petition_Cabo_Pulmo_Ramsar_%28eng%29.pdf.

5. Smithsonian National Museum of Natural History. (2016). Ocean Portal. *Cabo Pulmo Protected Area.* Available at: http://ocean.si.edu/cabo-pulmo-protected-area.

6. Ramsar Sites Information Service. (2016). *Parque Nacional Cabo Pulmo.* Available at: https://rsis.ramsar.org/ris/1778.

7. Octavio Aburto-Oropeza, Brad Erisman, Grantly Galland, Ismael Mascareñas-Osorio, Enric Sala, and Exequiel Ezcurra. (2011). Large Recovery of Fish Biomass in a No-Take Marine Reserve. *PLOS ONE*, August 12, 2011. Available at: http://dx.doi.org/10.1371/journal.pone.0023601.

8. Ibid.

9. Ibid.

10. Mexican national parks are managed by CONANP, the Cómision Nacional de Áreas Naturales Protegidas. Available at: http://www.conanp.gob.mx/index.php.

11. Image Source: Octavio Aburto.

12. Image Source: Martin Goebel.

13. Image Source: Martin Goebel.

14. Image Source: Martin Goebel.

15. Sula Vanderplank, Benjamin Wilder, and Exequiel Ezcurra (2014.) *Descubriendo la Biodiversidad Terrestre en la Región de Cabo Pulmo/ Uncovering the Dryland Biodiversity of the Cabo Pulmo Region.* Botanical Research Institute of Texas, Next Generation Sonoran Desert Researchers, and UC MEXUS. Available at: http://nextgensd.com/wp-content/uploads/2014/04/Cabo-Pulmo-Report_Final.pdf.

16. José Luis León De la Luz and Rachel Levin. (2012). *Pisonia Calafia (Nyctaginaceae)* Species Nova from the Baja California Peninsula, Mexico. *Acta Botanica Mexicana*, 101, 83–93. Available at: http://www1.inecol.edu.mx/abm/resumenes/Acta%20101(83-93).pdf.

17. Diario Oficial de la Federación. (2009). *Official Notice - Appendix: Programa de Conservacion y Manejo del Parque Nacional Cabo Pulmo* (Conservation and Management Plan for the Cabo Pulmo National

Park). Available at: http://www.dof.gob.mx/nota_detalle.php?codig o=5119488&fecha=13/11/2009.

18. Sylvia Earle. (2016). Mission Blue. *Transcription of Dr. Sylvia Earle's speech to the community of Cabo Pulmo on the Mission Blue Hope Spot Expedition to Cabo Pulmo Marine Park*, February 2016. Available at: https://www.mission-blue.org/2016/03/17413/.

Conclusion and Volume 2 Preview

Kreg Ettenger

The Caribbean is already seeing significant environmental impacts related to climate change, including deterioration of critical ecosystems like coral reefs, mangroves, seagrass beds, and coastal estuaries. Caribbean islands and coastal nations rely heavily on these ecosystems, and on the fish and other resources they provide, for food and income. Many of these nations also rely on various types of tourism, especially those related to marine and coastal recreation, such as boating, fishing, surfing, diving, and snorkeling. The vast majority of tourism infrastructure in these places, from airports and marinas to resorts and restaurants, are located in coastal areas, and will be especially vulnerable to the physical impacts expected (and already experienced) due to climate change. There is clearly a need to better understand the key issues that link the economic, ecological, social, and political aspects of tourism, resources, and climate change in this region.

As the essays and case studies in this volume suggest, marine tourism can have both positive and negative effects when it comes to climate change, environmental impacts, and the well-being of marine and coastal ecosystems and communities. On the one hand, marine tourism can share many of the negative aspects of land-based tourism, including the generation of greenhouse gases, rapid and poorly planned development, and the physical impacts of visitors on fragile and unique ecosystems. Such impacts have helped create the precarious situation that exists today in much of the Caribbean, as well as around the world.

On the other hand, marine tourism enthusiasts have begun to recognize the impacts that their activities can have on the places they love, and many are looking for solutions. They are also trying to find ways to survive the current and future impacts of climate change, adapting their activities, locations, and even entire industries to be more resilient and sustainable. They are working with local communities and global partners to find solutions that will protect the places they love and the habitats, ecosystems, and species that drive their passion for marine-related activities. In the end, those who head to the ocean for fun and relaxation might be the ones who lead us to new ways of successfully dealing with the effects of long-term climate change in the Caribbean and beyond.

In this volume, we explored the current state of some critical marine ecosystems, the condition of global and regional fisheries, and the potential for marine protected areas to conserve species and habitats, all within the context of climate change and marine tourism. In Volume 2, we look at three specific types of marine tourism, considering the impacts they are having on marine and coastal environments and communities as well as how they might play a larger role in mitigating the impacts of climate change. The three types of activities are marine recreation, including surfing, diving, and sport fishing; cruise tourism, including ports as well as shipboard activities; and yachting, sailing, and marinas. Each of these forms of marine tourism has its own complex set of impacts and benefits with respect to marine environments and coastal communities. Each also has the potential to lessen its climate impacts while protecting and preserving the marine habitats and coastal locations it depends on. The essays and case studies of the next volume explore these issues in depth, with examples of best practices that can help protect the Caribbean and other ocean-dependent places for generations to come.

Contributing Authors

Judith Castro Lucero

Judith Castro Lucero is currently serving her second term as director of the Cabo Pulmo Learning Center. In 2015, she was executive director of Friends of Cabo Pulmo, serving as Chair from 2001 to 2014. She also serves as president of the Advisory Board of Cabo Pulmo National Park. Judith is a native and long-term resident of Cabo Pulmo.

Luke Elder

Luke Elder is a master of environmental management candidate in the Yale School of Forestry, where he is studying corporate social responsibility and private sector solutions to climate change. Previous positions include program associate at The Ocean Foundation and field station manager for The Nature Conservancy.

Kreg Ettenger

Kreg Ettenger is associate professor of anthropology at the University of Maine, where he also directs the Maine Studies Program and Maine Folklife Center. Previously, he was founding chair of the Program in Tourism and Hospitality at the University of Southern Maine. He has a PhD in anthropology from Syracuse University.

Victor M. Galvan

Victor Galvan serves as ecological research coordinator at the Grupo Puntacana Foundation. He manages the coral restoration and internship programs, writes scientific publications, and serves as program coordinator for an Inter-American Development Bank technical collaboration award. He has a Master's degree from California State University, Los Angeles, with an emphasis on coral restoration.

Carlos Godinez-Reyes

Carlos Godinez-Reyes is director of Cabo Pulmo National Park and of Mexico's National Commission of Protected Natural Areas (CONANP). Previously, he was director of the Islas del Golfo de California in Baja California, as well as other reserves and parks. He has multiple degrees in wildlife science, animal biology, and veterinary medicine.

Martin Goebel

Martin Goebel is principal of Moebius Partners, LLC, and senior associate at Legacy Works Group. Previously he served as founding president of Sustainable Northwest, and as Mexico Director for The Nature Conservancy, Conservation International, and World Wildlife Fund. He has a degree in forestry from Oregon State University and a Master's degree from Texas A&M.

Craig Hays

Craig Hays is the founder and current board chairman of Turneffe Atoll Trust. In 1981, he and a small group of friends started Turneffe Flats Resort in Belize. Craig now spends most of his time overseeing Turneffe Flats and working on conservation issues at Turneffe Atoll and in Belize.

Marida Hines

Marida Hines is SeaWeb senior program manager for The Ocean Foundation, which works with donors to provide financial resources to marine conservation initiatives around the world. As part of her role, Marida manages two seafood sustainability programs. Marida has a BA from the University of Maryland College Park.

Jeremy Jackson

Jeremy Jackson holds emeritus positions at the Scripps Institution of Oceanography and the Smithsonian Institution. He studies threats and solutions to human impacts on the oceans and the ecology and evolution of tropical seas. His work on the collapse of coastal ecosystems was chosen by *Discover* magazine as the outstanding scientific achievement of 2001. He received his PhD in geology from Yale University.

Jake Kheel

Jake Kheel is vice-president of the Grupo Puntacana Foundation and oversees all social and environmental programs for Grupo Puntacana. Jake is also co-director and producer of *Death by a Thousand Cuts*, an award-winning documentary about deforestation on the island of Hispaniola. Jake has an MS in environmental management from Cornell University.

Kristin Kovalik

Kristin Kovalik is senior project manager at The Trust for Public Land in Montana. Previously, she was conservation director at Turneffe Atoll Trust, and served for over 16 years as central Oregon program director for The Trust for Public Land. She has degrees from the Pennsylvania State University and the University of Oregon.

Jen Levin

Jen Levin is sustainable seafood program manager for the Gulf of Maine Research Institute in Portland, Maine. Her focus is on chain-of-custody and verification systems that enable and motivate the sustainable seafood marketplace. Jen has a degree in wildlife ecology from the University of Wisconsin and an MBA from the University of Southern Maine.

Dawn M. Martin

Dawn Martin is COO, treasurer, and vice-chair of the Board for Ceres, a nonprofit organization advocating for sustainability leadership. She serves as a Trustee for the National Marine Sanctuary Foundation and sits on the board of The Ocean Foundation. Dawn received her J.D. from Loyola Law School, Los Angeles, and her BA in political science from Loyola Marymount University.

Dieter Rothenberger

Dieter Rothenberger heads the program "Integrated Climate Change Adaptation Strategies" for Deutsche Gesellschaft für Internationale Zusammenarbeit (GIZ). He has a Master's degree in development, environmental, and institutional economics from the University of Augsburg, and degrees and diplomas from the London School of Economics and Political Science, the University of London, and the University of Loughborough.

Daria Siciliano

Daria Siciliano is lead scientist for the Cuba Marine Research and Conservation Program of The Ocean Foundation, working closely with partners in the U.S. and Cuba. Dr. Siciliano is also a Research Associate at the Marine Science Institute of the University of California, Santa Cruz (UCSC). She holds a PhD in Biological Oceanography from UCSC.

Mark J. Spalding

Mark is president of The Ocean Foundation, advisor to the Rockefeller Ocean Strategy, and designer of the blue carbon offset program, SeaGrass Grow. Mark serves on the Sargasso Sea Commission and is a senior fellow at the Center for the Blue Economy, Middlebury Institute of International Studies. He holds a JD from Loyola Law School and a Master's degree in Pacific international affairs from UC San Diego.

Aria St. Louis

Aria St. Louis is a conservation geneticist and head of the Environment Division at the Ministry of Agriculture, Lands, Forestry, Fisheries and Environment in Grenada. Previously, she worked in the Department of Fisheries and Aquatic Sciences at the University of Florida. She holds a Master's degree in marine biology from the University of the West Indies (UWI Mona).

Rubén Torres

Ruben Torres is the Caribbean regional coordinator for Reef Check, and founder and president of Reef Check Dominican Republic. He is CEO of Torres Environmental Consulting, a member of the Global Coral Reef Monitoring Network, and a mentor for the UNEP Caribbean MPA Managers Network. Ruben has a PhD in marine biology from the University of Miami.

Sula Vanderplank

Sula is the interim director of research at the Botanical Research Institute of Texas (BRIT) and has studied the ecology of Baja California since 2005. She is the author of many botanical research papers and two books on the Baja California Peninsula, and was lead author of the 2014 report *Uncovering the Dryland Biodiversity of the Cabo Pulmo region.* Sula holds a PhD in plant ecology from the University of California, Riverside.

Shengxiao Yu

Shengxiao "Sole" Yu graduated from the University of Chicago with degrees in comparative human development and human rights. As an intern at Bodhi Surf School, Sole helped design their Travelers' Philanthropy Program. Currently Sole is Director of Partnerships at GlobeMed. She remains connected to Bodhi as a consultant and volunteer.

Chiara Zuccarino-Crowe

Chiara Zuccarino-Crowe is tourism and recreation coordinator for the Office of National Marine Sanctuaries within the U.S. National Oceanic and Atmospheric Administration. Chiara also serves on working groups of the U.S. Tourism Policy Council and the Federal Interagency Council on Outdoor Recreation. She holds an MS in fisheries and wildlife from Michigan State University.

Index

OTHER TITLES IN TOURISM AND HOSPITALITY MANAGEMENT COLLECTION

Betsy Bender Stringam, *Editor*

- *The Good Company: Sustainability in Hospitality, Tourism and Wine* by Robert Girling
- *Coastal Tourism, Sustainability, and Climate Change in the Caribbean, Volume I: Beaches and Hotels Edited* by Martha Honey with Samantha Hogenson
- *Coastal Tourism, Sustainability, and Climate Change in the Caribbean, Volume II: Supporting Activities Edited* by Martha Honey with Samantha Hogenson

FORTHCOMING TITLES

- *Catering and Convention Service Survival Guide in Hotels and Casinos* by Lisa Lynn Backus and Patti J. Shock
- *Marketing Essentials for Independent Lodging* by Pamela Lanier
- *Marine Tourism, Climate Change, and Resiliency in the Caribbean, Volume II Edited* by Kreg Ettenger with Samantha Hogenson

Announcing the Business Expert Press Digital Library

Concise e-books business students need for classroom and research

This book can also be purchased in an e-book collection by your library as

- a one-time purchase,
- that is owned forever,
- allows for simultaneous readers,
- has no restrictions on printing, and
- can be downloaded as PDFs from within the library community.

Our digital library collections are a great solution to beat the rising cost of textbooks. E-book scan be loaded into their course management systems or onto students' e-book readers. The **Business Expert Press** digital libraries are very affordable, with no obligation to buy in future years. For more information, please visit **www.businessexpertpress.com/librarians**. To set up a trial in the United States, please email **sales@businessexpertpress.com**.